Tarla Dalal *India's #1 Cookery Author*

· THE COMPLETE ·
ITALIAN COOK BOOK

EGGLESS
RECIPES
100% Vegetarian

S&C
SANJAY & CO.
MUMBAI

Fifth Printing : 2007

ISBN 10 :81-86469-52-4
ISBN 13 : 978-8-186469-52-1

Price Rs. 230/-

PUBLISHED & DISTRIBUTED BY :

SANJAY & COMPANY

353/A-1, Shah & Nahar Industrial Estate, Dhanraj Mill Compound, Lower Parel (W), Mumbai - 400 013. INDIA.
Tel. : (91-22) 2496 8068 • Fax : (91-22) 2496 5876 • E-mail : sanjay@tarladalal.com
Website : www.tarladalal.com

UK and USA customers can call us on :
UK : 02080029533   •   USA : 213-634-1406
For books, Membership on **tarladalal.com**, Subscription for **Cooking & More** and Recipe queries
Timing : 9.30 a.m. to 7.00 p.m. (IST), from Monday to Saturday
Local call charges applicable

Recipe Research & Production Design :
Pinky Dixit
Aarti Fedane
Jyoti Jain
Ushma Negandhi

Printed by :
Minal Sales Agnecies, Mumbai

Designed by :
Satyamangal Rege

Food Stylist :
Nitin Tandon

Photography :
Vinay Mahidhar

Illustrations :
Ganesh Tayde

OTHER BOOKS BY TARLA DALAL

INDIAN COOKING
Tava Cooking
Rotis & Subzis
Desi Khana
The Complete Gujarati Cook Book
Mithai
Chaat
Achaar aur Parathe
The Rajasthani Cookbook
Swadisht Subzian

WESTERN COOKING
The Chocolate Cookbook
Eggless Desserts
Mocktails & Snacks
Soups & Salads
Mexican Cooking
Easy Gourmet Cooking
Chinese Cooking
Easy Chinese Cooking
Thai Cooking
Sizzlers & Barbeques

GENERAL COOKING
Exciting Vegetarian Cooking
Microwave Cooking
Quick & Easy Cooking
Saatvik Khana
Mixer Cook Book
The Pleasures of Vegetarian Cooking
The Delights of Vegetarian Cooking
The Joys of Vegetarian Cooking
Cooking With Kids
Snacks Under 10 Minutes
Ice-Cream & Frozen Desserts
Desserts Under 10 Minutes
Entertaining
Microwave Snacks & Desserts

TOTAL HEALTH
Low Calorie Healthy Cooking
Pregnancy Cookbook
Baby and Toddler Cookbook
Cooking with 1 Teaspoon of Oil
Home Remedies
Delicious Diabetic Recipes
Fast Foods Made Healthy
Healthy Soups & Salads
Healthy Breakfast
Calcium Rich Recipes
Healthy Heart Cook Book
Forever Young Diet
Healthy Snacks
Iron Rich Recipes
Healthy Juices
Low Cholesterol Recipes
Good Food for Diabetes
Healthy Subzis
Healthy Snacks for Kids
High Blood Pressure Cook Book
Low Calorie Sweets
Nutritious Recipes for Pregnancy
Diabetic Snacks New
Zero Oil Rotis & Subzis New
Zero Oil Soups, Salads & Snacks New

MINI SERIES
Idlis & Dosas
Cooking under 10 minutes
Pizzas and Pastas
Fun Food for Children
Roz Ka Khana
Microwave - Desi Khana
T.V. Meals
Paneer
Parathas
Chawal
Dals
Sandwiches
Quick Cooking
Curries & Kadhis
Chinese Recipes
Jain Desi Khana
7 Dinner Menus
Jain International Recipes
Punjabi Subzis
Corn
Microwave Subzis
Baked Dishes New
Stir-Fry New

INTRODUCTION

Michaelangelo loved it.
The Pope smacks his lips for it.
The Mafia thrives on it.
Still confused??

From the land of art, architecture and fashion, we bring to your home, authentic Italian cooking. And we guarantee you even the Godfather loved it !!
Italy is not only famous for its tall, dusky and handsome men, but for its world renowned Pastas, Pizzas, Crostinis, Minestrone, Risottos and mouth-watering Tiramisu. These are amongst few of the recipes this book is about.

Every party goer's delight are the **starters**. Crostinis, Pizzettes (that are little individual pizzas) and flavourful Herbed Pizza Strips are among the few new variations which are sure to make every party a success.

The most essential part of Italian cuisine is the **soup**; a healthy, wholesome blend packed with vegetables, herbs, beans and pasta.

Make your own **Pizza**!!
Use the recipes for pizza bases, sauces and toppings to create the classic Pizza Margherita and the new Pizza Pesto Sandwich, or you can get creative and make your own concoction.

Pastas and **Sauces** are every dieter's favourite. Make your own Pastas or simply use the ready-made ones to savour old favorites like Garlic Basil Ravioli with Alfredo Sauce or Spaghetti Puttanesca. For an absolutely new dinner idea, try the Spaghetti Verdi.

After all this, if you are still hungry then treat your taste buds to a Risotto or a Gnocchi for the main dish.
If you have a sweet tooth then, there's the irresistible selection of Italy's most loved **desserts** such as Tiramisu and Zuccoto.

Use the glossary to familiarize yourself with the ingredients used in Italian cooking. Whether you are a beginner or an expert cook, we hope this book guides you through terrific cooking.
So put on your chef cap and whip up your own masterpiece.

A vivere la dolce vita! (Here's to living the sweet life.)

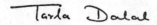

ITALIAN REGIONAL COOKING

Italy is a country of changing climates and landscapes and so its cooking varies according to the region from which a particular dish comes.

The most significant divide for Italian cuisine is that between the industrial north and the poorer south. The north with its fertile plains, its mountains and lakes, produces good quality wines and dairy foods. By contrast, the sunnier, rockier south is home to olive trees, tomatoes and fresh herbs.

Although there are regional differences in the cuisine, they do have features in common:- the ingredients are fresh, the techniques are simple, the recipes are traditional and the cooking is home style.

Piedmont

The name means "at the foot of the mountain" which the area is, bordering on both France and Switzerland.

The food is substantial, peasant type fare and garlic features strongly in recipes. Gnocchi and rice are eaten in larger quantity than pasta.

Lombardy

Lombardy is the home of the **risotto** and almost every Lombardian housewife has her own special way of making it. There are many outstanding culinary specialties, particularly in and around the city of Milan. **Milanese risotto** is justifiably famous all over the world, known for its distinctive flavour and creamy texture.

Trentino-alto adige

This is an area of mountains, rich green valleys and lakes. There is a strong German influence present in the cuisine. The foods are robust and basic. Pasta, soups and casseroles are very popular.

Veneto

The illustrious port of **Venice** is the centre of this region and holds the key to the cuisine of the whole area. The cooking of Veneto can be reduced to four basic elements - rice, beans, gnocchi and soups. Vibrant red, green and yellow peppers and aubergines are extensively used in the food of Veneto. Rice is the staple cereal and is frequently served in the form of a risotto. Finally, we should thank the Venetians for coffee, because it was Venetian sailors who imported the coffee bean from the East and the Italians who taught us the art of making **expresso and cappuccino.**

Liguria

Often called the " Italian Riveria", this region is rich in natural resources and has abundance of herbs, vegetables, olives and fruits. The Genoese are excellent cooks and the cuisine from this region is considered to be among the best in Italian food. Ligurian cooking is characterised by the distinctive flavour of freshly picked basil. This herb is used extensively in the cooking of the area but is perhaps best known for its inclusion in pesto, the classic Genoese sauce. **Pesto** is a pounded mixture of basil, garlic, olive oil, pine nuts and parmesan cheese. It appears in many different forms throughout the region. **Minestrone** is another specialty of this region and the Genoese claim to have created it.

Liguria is reputed to be the birthplace of **"ravioli"**, a pillow shaped pasta.

Fresh herbs are widely used in many dishes including the famous pizzas - their aroma is unmistakable.

Emilia-Romagna

This region is renowned for its pasta dishes. The varieties of pasta are numerous like tortellini, lasagne, tagliatelle etc. The pasta of Emilia-Romagna are almost always served with thick vegetable sauces.

Probably the most famous product to come from this region is **Parmesan cheese**. It takes its name from the town of Parma. **Balsamic Vinegar** is another specialty of this region.

Tuscany

Vegetables, olive oil, herbs and wine form the bulk of the Tuscan diet. Tuscan dishes are aptly described as traditional, plain and wholesome, for food is generally served as simply as possible.

Florence which lies in this region boasts of a wide variety of specialties. Another excellent product is the **olive oil** from Lucca in the north of Tuscany.

Chianti, the most famous wine to come from Italy, belongs to the Tuscan region.

Umbria / Marches

Vegetables, fruits and olives grow abundantly in this region. Mushrooms, peas, beans and onions are also grown. Olives from **Trevi** are pressed to make fine quality **Trevi olive oil.**

Umbria / Marches is blessed with a cuisine with strong family traditions and many fine dishes have come from this area. Pasta features predominantly all over the region.

Lazio

With the city of **Rome** at its centre, the region of Lazio lies in the centre of the country. The cuisine of Rome has drawn influences from each of the distinctive cuisines of north and south Italy. But it has also retained a character of its own. Roman cooking is hearty, robust and highly seasoned. Fettuccine, cannelloni, spaghetti and gnocchi are eaten in large quantities.

Ricotta cheese is also widely used in Roman cooking for both sweets and savouries.

Abruzzi Molise

The cuisine here is deeply traditionally using local cheeses from the mountain areas. Garlic is used extensively in most recipes. Peppers, aubergines and tomatoes are grown in the fertile valleys and appear in many local dishes.

Campania

Neapolitan cuisine is arguably the most popular of all cuisines. **Naples** is the home of pasta dishes, served with a splendid tomato sauce (with many variations). **Pizza** is said to have been created in Naples.

The main characteristics of southern cuisine are tubular pasta, the use of olive oil for cooking and the extensive use of tomatoes and garlic, particularly in sauces. This part of Italy is considered poor at least in relation to the north. The basic foodstuffs are often described as humble, but the Neapolitans transform them into a vast number of different dishes.

This region is also famous for its cooking cheese **mozzarella**.

Southern Italy is more than proud of its **ice-creams and sorbets** for these were invented here.

Puglia (Apulia) and Basilicata

Many of the excellent pasta dishes belong to these regions. Mushrooms are abundantly found here and are always added to the local pizzas. Apulians are also very fond of savoury breads made from pizza dough. **Calzone** is said to have originated here.

Calabria

This is the "toe" of Italy, where orange and lemon groves flourish along with olive trees and a profusion of vegetables.

In true southern tradition, the many forms of pasta are the staple of the local cuisine. Pasta dishes are layered or served with heavy vegetable sauces. Pasta is also used in soups. Pastries, cakes and other confections are popular throughout Calabria.

Sicily

This is the largest island in the Mediterranean sea and the cuisine is based mainly on fruits and vegetables.

It is basically a peasant style of cooking with bread and pasta forming the staple diet.

Groves of citrus fruit, olives and grapes can be seen all over the island.

Indeed, Sicily is often described as a "paradise" for the vine. Sicilians love desserts, cakes and especially ice-cream.

Cassatta and other ice-creams from Sicily are famous all over the world.

Sardinia

It is the second largest of the Mediterranean islands. The cooking is basically peasant style. Pasta, breads and local cheeses feature often in their cuisine.

Italian CULINARY REGIONS

COMMONLY USED INGREDIENTS

Cheeses

a. *__Mozzarella__* - This cheese has a soft texture, it is mild white and has a delicate flavour. It can be used for salads and provides a tangy layer in baked dishes. It is also a popular topping for pizzas for its ability to melt and to produce strings of cheese once a pizza is baked and a slice is cut apart.

b. *__Cooking cheese__* - A variety of cheese which is a blend of two or more cheeses in varying proportions, it is blended so as to melt readily while cooking.

c. *__Parmesan__* - A mature, hard cow's milk cheese. Excellent for topping on soups and pasta. Originally from the city of Parma, the finest and most authentic cheese has the "Parmigiano Reggiano" seal stamped on its hard rind and has a flaky, dry texture when cut. It is available pre-shredded and in wedges. It is also used classically as an ingredient of pesto.

d. *__Feta cheese__* - Feta is a sharp tasting, white and firm cheese made from goat's milk. It is delicious when sprinkled over salads. Feta cheese is similar in texture to cottage cheese, apart from being more saltier.

e. *__Ricotta__* - This is a fresh and creamy soft cheese similar to cottage cheese (paneer), but with a sweeter flavour. Ricotta cheese retains its texture when heated, making it ideal for stuffing pies or as a layer in lasagna as shown in the recipe of Spinach & Ricotta Pie, page 59. Ricotta is also used in desserts such as Chocolate Ricotta Torte, recipe on page 128.

d. *__Cheddar cheese__* - One of the most popular and well known cheeses of the world which is made from cow's milk. It can be white or yellow in colour and is hard and smooth in texture. It imparts a good flavour to pasta recipes and can be used as a substitute for Parmesan cheese.

f. *__Mascarpone__* - This is a rich, soft cheese, smooth and mild in flavour and has originated in northern Italy. Similar to cream cheese, it is ideal for making cheese based desserts. Mascarpone is the cheese used in the popular Italian dessert, Tiramisu, recipe on page 116.

g. *__Processed cheese__* - It is a "pasteurised cheese" (generally a blend of one or more cheeses of the same variety or two or more varieties) which is readily available in the market. Use in any recipe, stating "cheese" or "table cheese".

h. *__Cheese spread__* - It is a kind of processed cheese used as a topping for several recipes. It is available in several flavours like plain, garlic, pepper, cumin etc.

i. *__Flavoured cheese__* - This includes an array of cheeses available at gourmet stores like herb flavoured cheeses, paprika cheese, pepper cheese, garlic cheese, cumin flavoured cheese. These can be made at home by mixing the desired flavouring ingredients like paprika, garlic etc. with mozzarella or processed cheese.

Herbs

a. ***Basil*** - Basil belongs to the 'tulsi' family. It is available in dried form or as fresh basil leaves which are packed and sold by some vegetable vendors. If you use dried basil, use only half the quantity specified in the recipe as dried herbs are more concentrated.

b. ***Oregano*** - Also known as wild marjoram, it is available in two forms - fresh and dried. Dried oregano is very concentrated and stronger in flavour and should be used sparingly. It combines very well in Italian cooking in pasta and pizza sauces, especially tomato - based dishes.

c. ***Parsley*** - A family of aromatic herbs, used to flavour and garnish several recipes. The most commonly available kind of parsley has flat smooth leaves and the other is the curled parsley which has bright green leaves and is used mostly as a garnish. It is available both in dried and fresh form. Fresh parsley is sold in packets by some vegetable vendors. Coriander is a part of the parsley family.

d. ***Thyme*** - A herb which belongs to the mint family. The leaves are used in fresh or dry form. It is highly aromatic and should therefore be used sparingly. Leaves of carom (ajwain) can be used as substitute for thyme.

e. ***Rosemary*** - An aromatic shrub native to Mediterranean countries, whose evergreen leaves, are either used fresh or dried as flavouring. Rosemary has a fresh, sweet flavour that can be very strong. It is excellent for breads such as the Smoked Pepper & Cheese bread, recipe on page 65. Rosemary is most often sprinkled and baked on focaccia bread.

f. ***Chives*** - Delicate chive stems have a very mild onion flavour and a bright green colour. They can be used in almost any food in which a mild onion flavoured taste is desired. Fresh chives have a better flavour than dried.

g. ***Mixed Herbs*** - There are several recipes indicating the use of mixed dried herbs. It consists of equal proportions of dried oregano, thyme, basil and parsley mixed together. The mixture can be prepared or can be bought as mixed herbs from grocery shops.

Other Ingredients

a. ***Olive Oil*** - Olive oil, which is the heart of so many Italian dishes, has its own characteristic flavour, which enhances and complements several pizza and pasta recipes. Olive oil is sold under various classifications– "Virgin" (extra fine or fine) or "Pure" (i.e. mixed virgin and refined olive oil). However, olive oil can be substituted with refined oil in case of non-availability.

b. ***Yeast*** - Two types of yeast are available in the market—fresh and dried. Both types can be used for making of pizza bases. Fresh yeast should always be stored in an air-tight container and refrigerated. Whenever dried yeast is used, it should be half the quantity of fresh yeast mentioned in the recipe. As it is a more concentrated yeast, it also needs to be activated in lukewarm water or milk before using in a recipe.

c. ***Jalapeno Chillies*** - A pickled variety of a large green Mexican chilli which is readily available at many grocery stores.

d. ***Chilli Flakes*** - Chilli flakes are made from dried red chillies which are roughly pounded to form chilli flakes. The seeds of the chillies are removed before pounding the chillies. Chilli flakes or paprika flakes are readily available at grocery shops.

e. ***Pine nuts (Chilgoza)*** - They are the small edible seeds of the stone pine. They can be eaten raw, but are usually roasted for using in recipes. In India, they are used for garnishes. Pine nuts are also used for making the pesto but can be substituted by walnuts in case of non-availability.

f. ***Seasoning Cube*** - This consists of salt and artificial flavours and seasoning. It is easily available at all grocery stores and is an alternative to making stocks for soups.

g. ***Olives*** - They are small oval fruits of the olive tree, widely cultivated in the Mediterranean region. The fruit ripens from green to black. Olives are pitted (deseeded) and pickled in brine and bottled. Green olives are often stuffed with red pimentos before being pickled.

h. ***Sea Salt*** - Sea salt resembles coarse white crystals. It is salt in its unrefined state after it has been obtained from sea water. Sea salt is used in cooking in the process of "pickling".

ALL ABOUT PASTA

Pasta is a generic term for many products which are made from a dough of durum wheat flour or semolina. Here, there are two kinds of pasta - those you can buy and those you must make. A good Italian cook would never hesitate to do both. All kinds of dried pasta are commonly referred to as "Macaroni" and this includes all shapes and flavours. They are cooked in water and served with a sauce and sometimes with nothing more than a little butter and a sprinkling of grated cheese.

Fresh or home-made pasta such as ravioli, lasagne, fettuccine etc. are time consuming to make but the efforts are always worthwhile.

Whichever pasta you use, be it fresh or dried pasta, be sure to get the best quality you can.

VARIETIES OF PASTA

a. **_Alphabet_** - Small alphabet shaped pasta, ideally used for soups.

b. **_Angel Hair Pasta (Capelli d' Angelo)_** - Very thin strands of pasta, usually sold in coils.

c. **_Cannelloni_** - Smaller sheets of pasta (like lasagne) that are cooked in water, stuffed with a filling mixture and rolled lightly like a cylinder. These are placed on a baking dish topped with a sauce and baked.

d. **_Conchiglie (shells)_** - Ridged shaped shells ranging in size from small bite sized shells to large ones.

e. **_Farfalle (Bow ties)_** - Butterfly shaped pasta.

f. **_Fettuccine (Tagliatelle)_** - Long flat ribbon shaped pasta usually about 6 mm. (¼") wide. It is available dried as plain, spinach, tomato or whole wheat fettuccine. It can also be made fresh.

g. **_Fusilli (Spirals)_** - Small pasta in the shape of spindles or corkscrews.

h. **_Lasagne_** - Sheets of fresh or dried pasta, usually cooked layered with filling and sauce and baked. Lasagne sheets can be brought ready-made or can be freshly made. This pasta can be flavoured with a variety of vegetable purées like spinach, tomato, carrot or several fresh or dried herbs or saffron.

i. **_Linguine_** - A flat, strand like pasta, much thinner than fettuccine.

j. **_Macaroni_** - Long or short cut tubes of pasta which may be ridged or elbow shaped.

k. **_Penne_** - Short, thick tubes of pasta with diagonal cut ends.

l. **_Ravioli_** - Fresh pasta which is filled with a sweet or savoury mixture. The filling is encased between 2 sheets of thin pasta, which is cooked in water and served with a sauce.

m. **_Spaghetti_** - Long strands of pasta. These can be fine, medium or thick strands. Spaghetti is the most commonly available pasta.

n. **_Tortellini_** - Similar to ravioli, but with a twisted irregular shape.

o. **_Vermicelli_** - Fine slender strands of pasta, which can be long or even short strands.

Some of these pasta shapes have been identified in the picture below.

1. Penne
2. Dried Tortellini
3. Olive Oil
4. Dried Lasagne sheets
5. Chilli flakes
6. Black Olives
7. Flavoured cheese
8. Cooking cheese
9. Mozzarella
10. Grated Parmesan Cheese
11. Spaghetti
12. Macaroni
13. Farfalle (Bow ties)
14. Fusilli (Spirals)
15. Dried Ravioli
16. Fettuccine
17. Elbow Macaroni
18. Green Olives
19. Sun-Dried Tomatoes

INDEX

STARTERS

SOUPS

SALADS

PIZZAS AND BREADS

HOME-MADE PASTA

QUICK READY-MADE PASTA

RICE AND GNOCCHI

DESSERTS

BASIC RECIPES

STARTERS

"Antipasto" as they are called in Italy, literally means "before the pasta" and is served as a starter or an appetiser. This section contains recipes of crostinis, vegetable dishes, fried or baked morsels, just large enough to take the edge off a diner's hunger without being too filling. With so many fresh ingredients available, it is easy to create delicious starters that are the perfect introduction to an Italian meal. The ideas in this section are an inspiration to cook and a treat to eat.

BRUSCHETTA WITH TOMATO & BASIL

Picture on page 26

"Crostini", a classic combination of bread, olive oil and garlic which has been enjoyed for hundreds of years, is also called "bruschetta" around Rome. Although unique to Italy, similar toasts are eaten in Greece, France and in particular Spain.
Good bruschetta relies on the quality of the olive oil and the amount of garlic used. The former can never be too good while the latter should not be restrained. Cubes of firm ripe red tomatoes marinated in olive oil, combined with fresh aromatic basil leaves topped on crispy bruschetta, are starters that can liven up any dinner party!

 Preparation time : 10 minutes. Cooking time : 5 minutes. Makes 8 to 10 pieces.

8 to 10 slices of French bread [20 mm. (¾") thick]
1 tablespoon olive oil
1 clove garlic, crushed

For the topping
3 to 4 medium tomatoes
1 large clove garlic, chopped
½ tablespoon fresh basil leaves, chopped
½ teaspoon dried oregano
3 tablespoons olive oil
salt and freshly ground pepper to taste

For the topping
1. Cut each tomato into 2 pieces vertically and gently remove all the seeds and pulp.
2. Chop the firm tomatoes into small pieces, add in all the other ingredients and mix well.
3. Keep aside for at least 10 to 15 minutes. Drain out the excess liquid.

How to proceed

1. Brush some olive oil and garlic onto each French bread slice and bake in a pre-heated oven at 180°C (360°F) for 3 to 4 minutes till each is lightly toasted.
2. Spoon out the topping mixture generously onto each slice and serve immediately.

HANDY TIP If French bread is not available, you can use toasted bread. Preferably use thicker slices so that they can soak up all the juices.

ROASTED BELL PEPPER CROSTINI
Picture on page 26

Crostini are small toasts topped with a variety of ingredients and are served as appetisers. They are native to Tuscany and have several classic toppings to choose from.

This one consists of caramelised peppers and olives that are bound with cheese and topped on crusty French bread.

Good crusty bread is the single most essential ingredient for this recipe.

This is perhaps the best crostini of all and is perfect for serving with drinks before a meal.

Preparation time : 15 minutes. Cooking time : 25 minutes. Makes 8 to 10 pieces.

8 to 10 slices of French bread [20 mm (¾" thick)]

For the topping

1 cup red, green and yellow peppers, cut into short strips
½ cup finely chopped onions
1 large clove garlic, grated
½ teaspoon sugar
¼ cup mozzarella cheese or cooking cheese, cut into short strips
4 stuffed green olives, sliced
2 tablespoons olive oil or oil
salt and freshly ground pepper to taste

For the topping

1. Heat the olive oil and sauté the peppers, onions and garlic over very low heat till they caramelise lightly.
2. Add the sugar, salt, pepper and sauté for 2 to 3 minutes.
3. Remove from the flame and cool completely.

How to proceed

1. Top the pepper mixture, cheese strips and olives generously onto the French bread slices, arranging them decoratively.
2. Bake in a pre-heated oven at 200°C (400°F) for 3 to 4 minutes or until the cheese has melted.
   Serve hot.

SPICY CHEESE & HERB POTATO WEDGES

Potatoes are most commonly eaten in the northern part of Italy. Fried, mashed, sautéed or steamed. They are cooked in innumerable ways and flavoured with many different flavourings like thyme, oregano, garlic, onions, olive oil, tomatoes. The addition of potatoes to any dish makes it a substantial one.
This recipe of baked potato wedges flavoured with aromatic herbs and cheese is delightful, both as a snack and as an accompaniment to the main meal.

Preparation time : 5 minutes. Cooking time : 30 minutes. Serves 4.

4 large potatoes, cut into French fries (with the skin)
2 tablespoons melted butter
1 tablespoon olive oil or oil
2 cloves garlic, grated
½ teaspoon dried oregano
½ teaspoon dried rosemary
½ teaspoon crushed pepper
4 tablespoons grated cheese
salt to taste

1. Mix the melted butter, olive oil, garlic, oregano, rosemary, crushed pepper and salt in a bowl.
2. Add the potatoes and toss well so as to completely coat with the mixture.
3. Place the potatoes in a baking tray in a single layer and bake in a pre-heated oven at 200°C (400°F) for 20 to 25 minutes or until the potatoes are cooked, stirring once in between.
4. Sprinkle the cheese on top and mix well and bake for another 3 to 4 minutes.
Serve immediately.

HANDY TIP The wedges are best when prepared and cooked close to serving time.

HERBED PIZZA STRIPS

This style of flat bread is eaten all around the Mediterranean regions. Freshly made bread is rolled out and cut into thick strips, brushed generously with olive oil, flavoured with plenty of garlic and just the right amount of herbs sprinkled on top. Baked in the oven till the crust is crisp and golden brown on the outside and soft and chewy inside.

Leftover scraps of pizza dough can be used for this recipe. It is best when freshly baked, while still warm and fragrant to eat as a snack or to go with a meal.

Preparation time : 5 minutes. Cooking time : 15 minutes. Makes 8 pieces.

½ recipe basic pizza base, page 134

To be mixed into a herb topping
3 teaspoons olive oil or oil
1 teaspoon garlic paste
1 teaspoon (dried) mixed herbs
½ teaspoon crushed pepper
salt to taste

Other ingredients
olive oil or oil for greasing and glazing

How to proceed
1. Place the pizza base on a greased baking tray.
2. Using a pastry brush, brush the herb topping on top of the pizza base.
3. Cut the pizza base into 75 mm. x 37 mm. (3" x 1½") thick strips using a sharp knife or a dough cutter. Prick with a fork at regular intervals.
4. Bake in a pre-heated oven at 220°C (430°F) for 10 to 15 minutes or till the base is evenly browned.
5. Glaze the hot pizza strips with olive oil.
6. Warm the pizza strips in an oven before serving.
   Serve hot with soup.

FRIED MOZZARELLA STICKS

Mozzarella is synonymous for cheese in Italy. Naples is the city of origin for this cow's milk cheese characterised with a chewy, stringy texture.

Sticks of mozzarella cheese are coated with a herbed flour batter, rolled in bread crumbs and then deep fried in smoking hot oil to make this tongue tickling starter! Eat these sticks as soon as they are fried to get the taste of melted cheese. Coat the cheese sticks completely with the flour batter and bread crumbs to prevent the cheese from oozing out of the covering when it is being fried.

This recipe is an absolute hit with everyone who eats it !

I like to serve these sticks with the tomato and red wine sauce but you can also serve them with tomato sauce or ketchup.

 Preparation time : 10 minutes. Cooking time : 15 minutes. Makes 20 to 25 pieces.

250 grams mozzarella cheese

For the batter
½ cup plain flour (maida)
¼ cup cornflour
½ teaspoon dried oregano

½ teaspoon chilli flakes
salt to taste

Other ingredients
2 cups dried bread crumbs
oil for deep frying

For serving
½ recipe tomato and red wine sauce, page 113

1. Cut the mozzarella cheese into sticks (like French fries) and freeze.
2. Combine all the ingredients for the batter in a bowl and make a thick batter using approximately ½ cup of water.
3. Dip each cheese stick into the batter and coat with a thick layer of bread crumbs, pressing them firmly. Refrigerate for ½ hour.
4. Deep fry a few pieces at a time in very hot oil for a few seconds till golden brown.
5. Serve immediately with the tomato and red wine sauce.

 You can double coat the sticks with the batter and crumbs so that the cheese does not ooze out of the covering. The oil should be very hot and the sticks should be deep-fried insert over a high flame.

PIZZETTA SQUARES

Picture on page 25

Pizzettas are little individual pizzas from Sicily. They are nothing more than tiny pizza bread squares. Here they are given a whole new appeal by topping with freshly made sun-dried tomato pesto, fresh green basil leaves and caramelised onions. Of course, no pizza ever seems complete without mozzarella cheese.

You can use ready-made mini pizza bases for this recipe, but we all know nothing tastes as good as home-made bread.

This is one of my favourite snacks. It tastes great with lots of mozzarella and crusty Italian bread.

 Preparation time : 15 minutes. Cooking time : 30 minutes. Makes 20 squares.

1 recipe basic pizza base, page 134
1 recipe sun-dried tomato pesto, page 141
2 large onions, thinly sliced
¼ cup fresh basil leaves, chopped
1 cup mozzarella cheese or cooking cheese, grated
1 teaspoon olive oil or oil
salt to taste
oil for greasing

1. Place one pizza base on a greased baking tray. Prick with a fork at regular intervals.
2. Bake in a pre-heated oven at 200°C (400°F) for 10 minutes or until the base is evenly browned.
3. Repeat for the remaining dough to make one more pizza base.
4. Cut each pizza base into 10 pieces approximately 50 mm. x 50 mm. (2" x 2").
5. Heat the olive oil in a pan, add the onions and salt and sauté till the onions are golden brown. Remove and keep aside.
6. Spread a little sun-dried tomato pesto on each of the pizza base squares.
7. Top each pizza square with the onions, basil and grated cheese. Bake in a pre-heated oven at 200°C (400°F) for 3 to 4 minutes or till the cheese has melted. Serve hot.

**1. Penne with Spring Onions,
   Corn & Red Pepper,** *page 97*
2. Pizzetta Squares, *page 23*

OLIVE CREAM CHEESE DIP

Picture on page 86

Olives are almost always served in Italy, a custom that comes down from Roman times. Pickled olives have been served as a snack or after a meal along with cheese for hundreds of years.

A combination of truly authentic Italian flavours, cream cheese, perked up with olives and celery make this delightful recipe.

If you make the dip in advance, store it in the refrigerator. Mix in a tablespoon of cream if the dip becomes too dry when serving.

If the paneer is not fresh and creamy, try using a little cream and smoothen the paneer by making a fine purée in the blender.

There is no limit to what you can serve this dip with. For example, crackers, potato chips, toast, pieces of fresh vegetables — the combinations are endless and of course divine! You can even use this dip as a sandwich spread.

 Preparation time : 10 minutes. No cooking. Makes ¾ cup.

½ cup fresh paneer (cottage cheese), grated
1 tablespoon fresh cream
2 tablespoons cheese spread
6 to 8 black olives, deseeded and chopped
1 tablespoon chopped celery
salt to taste

1. Combine the paneer, fresh cream and cheese spread in a bowl and mix well till it is smooth and creamy.
2. Add all the other ingredients and mix again. Refrigerate.

Serve with crackers, breadsticks and vegetable sticks like carrots, celery, capsicum etc.

1. **Neapolitan Potato Salad**, *page 42*
2. **Broccoli Soup**, *page 36*
3. **Roasted Bell Pepper Crostini**, *page 19*
4. **Bruschetta with Tomato & Basil**, *page 18*

MUSHROOM OLIVE CROSTINI

In almost all of Italy, crostini means any toast or buttered bread presented at the beginning of the meal as an appetiser.
But in Florence, crostini is bread spread with this mushroom olive mixture.
Serve these tiny rounds of toasted bread with a tangy mustard flavoured mushroom and olive topping.
You can even add peppers, baby corn or any other vegetables you like along with the mushrooms. But make it fresh and eat it quickly.

 Preparation time : 10 minutes. Cooking time : 15 minutes. Makes 12 pieces.

6 large bread slices
butter for cooking

For the topping
1 cup mushrooms, finely chopped
2 tablespoons onion, finely chopped
½ green chilli, finely chopped
2 teaspoons plain flour (maida)
½ cup milk
1 tablespoon grated cheese
¼ teaspoon french style mustard
4 to 6 black olives, deseeded and chopped
1 tablespoon butter
salt and pepper to taste

For the toppping
1. Heat the butter in a pan, add the onion and green chilli and sauté till the onion is translucent.
2. Add the mushrooms and plain flour and sauté for a further 2 minutes.
3. Gradually add the milk, while stirring continuously so that no lumps form. Bring to a boil.
4. Add the cheese, mustard, black olives, salt and pepper and mix well. Allow it to cool and keep aside.

How to proceed

1. Cut the bread into 50 mm. (2") diameter circles, using a cookie cutter. You will get about 12 circles.
2. Lightly butter each bread circle on one side.
3. Arrange the buttered bread circles on a baking tray and bake in a pre-heated oven at 180°C (360°F) for 2 to 3 minutes.
4. Spread the topping mixture generously on top of each bread circle. Bake in a pre-heated oven at 180°C (360°F) for 2 to 3 minutes.
   Serve hot.

ONION & BLACK PEPPER GRISSINI

There are many stories as to the origin of grissini (Italian for breadsticks). One favourite story is that a baker in Turin in the 1660s shaped them out of bread dough in response to a request by the local Savoy duke who suffered from indigestion.

This recipe of grissini is made without using yeast and is very quick to prepare. Store them in an air-tight container. They may need to be refreshed in a hot oven before serving.

These onion and pepper flavoured sticks are great to serve with soup or a dip or just to be eaten on their own.

 Preparation time : 10 minutes. Cooking time : 25 minutes. Makes 20 to 25 pieces.

1 cup plain flour (maida)
1 level teaspoon baking powder
½ cup grated cheese
⅓ cup chopped onion
3½ tablespoons melted butter
1 teaspoon crushed pepper
salt to taste

1. Heat 1 teaspoon of butter in a pan and sauté the onions in it till they are translucent.
2. In a bowl, combine all the ingredients and knead gently into a dough, using water.
3. Divide the dough into 3 equal parts and roll out each portion into a 6 mm. (¼") thick sheet. Prick with a fork at regular intervals.
4. Cut into strips of 12 mm. (½") width and 60 mm. (2¼") length.
5. Place them on baking trays and bake in a pre-heated oven at 180°C (360°F) for 15 to 20 minutes or till they are golden brown.
   Store in an air-tight container.

PIZZELLE WITH MOZZARELLA & OLIVES

Pizzelle resemble small bite sized calzones. I have stuffed these with some Italian favourites, cheese and olives, spiked with basil and pepper.
Pizzelles are an example of a by-product becoming very popular in its own right.
It was originally made using left-over dough (usually pizza or bread dough) folded around a tasty morsel (probably left-overs as well). Pizzelle are either deep fried or baked and are always served hot.
Seal the ends of the pizzelles very tightly so as to prevent the cheese from oozing out while they are being baked.
Serve them hot with a spicy tomato sauce.

 Preparation time : 15 minutes. Cooking time : 20 minutes. Makes 15 pieces.

1 recipe basic pizza base, page 134

To be mixed into a filling
½ cup stuffed green olives, chopped
½ cup mozzarella cheese or cooking cheese, grated
10 fresh basil leaves, chopped
½ teaspoon crushed pepper

olive oil or oil to grease and glaze

1. Divide the pizza base into 2 equal portions. Roll out each portion into a sheet of 150 mm. x 150 mm. (6" x 6") and 6 mm. (¼ ") thickness.
2. Cut out 6 circles of 75 mm. (3") diameter using a cookie cutter. Roll out the scraps of dough to make more circles.
3. Place the filling mixture on the centre of each circle and fold into half, sealing the edges tightly, using a little water.
4. Place on a greased baking tray and bake in a pre-heated oven at 200°C (400°F) for 15 minutes or till golden brown.
5. Brush with olive oil and serve hot.

 HANDY TIP   You can even deep fry the pizzelles, if you do not want to bake them. Remember to fry them over a medium flame so that they cook well on the insides too.

R I V I E R A   L O A F

This delicious cheese, olive and sun-dried tomato topped bread is perfect with pasta and would also double up as a welcome appetiser!
Cut this loaf into bite size pieces. It is perfect for parties, buffets and to serve with pre-dinner drinks.

 Preparation time : 5 minutes. Cooking time : 5 minutes. Serves 4.

4 nos. hot dog rolls

To be mixed into a topping
10 nos. sun-dried tomatoes, page 142, soaked and chopped
1 tablespoon garlic, chopped
1 tablespoon chilli flakes
1 cup cooking cheese or mozzarella cheese, grated
8 nos. black olives, deseeded and sliced
8 nos. stuffed green olives, sliced
1 tablespoon olive oil or oil
salt to taste

1. Cut each hot dog roll lengthwise into two.
2. Divide the topping into 8 equal portions.
3. Spread each portion of the topping on each cut side of the hot dog roll.
4. Bake in a pre-heated oven at 200°C (400°F) for 2 to 3 minutes or until the cheese has just melted.
5. Cut into pieces and serve hot.

HANDY TIP If you are using sun-dried tomatoes preserved in olive oil, you do not have to soak them in water. Just drain the excess olive oil out.

SOUPS

"Zuppa" as they are called in Italian are a very important part of the cuisine. Many of the soups constitute a whole meal particularly those containing heavy ingredients like beans and pasta. All the ingredients for soup are chosen carefully when they are in season and at the peak of their perfection. There are certain regional classics too, like in the north of Italy, rice based soups are popular whereas tomato, garlic and pasta soups are typical of the south. Minestrone is known worldwide, but the best known version probably comes from Milan.. All are full of flavour and totally satisfying.

PESTO MINESTRONE

Minestrone is probably known worldwide. Every region and every cook in Italy have their own version and personal view about minestrone. The word grew out of "minestra" which means a broth and the one thing all minestrones tend to have in common is that they are hearty vegetable soups.

The single ingredient most frequently used is beans. Short pasta or rice may also be added.

The best known version comes from Milan. This version has plenty of vegetables and the pesto lends a slightly nutty flavour to the soup. This soup is best served just as it is completed. You can make the pesto sauce ahead, but add it while finishing the soup.

 Preparation time : 15 minutes. Cooking time : 15 minutes. Serves 4.

½ cup onions, finely chopped
¼ cup celery, finely chopped
½ cup carrots, finely chopped
1 cup zucchini, sliced (optional)
1 clove garlic, finely chopped
¼ cup shell pasta (conchiglie)
2 tomatoes, blanched, peeled and finely chopped
2 tablespoons baked beans (canned)
2 tablespoons olive oil or oil
salt and pepper to taste

To be pounded into a pesto
1 tablespoon fresh basil leaves
2 to 3 walnut halves
1 tablespoon olive oil or oil

For serving
4 tablespoons parmesan cheese or processed cheese, grated

1. Heat the olive oil in a pan, add the onions, celery, carrots, zucchini and garlic and sauté till the onions turn translucent.
2. Add the pasta, tomatoes, baked beans and 4 cups of hot water and simmer till the pasta is just cooked (approx. 8 to 10 minutes).
3. Add the salt, pepper and the prepared pesto and mix well.
   Serve hot, sprinkled with parmesan cheese.

BEAN & PASTA SOUP

A dish with proud Mediterranean origins, this soup is a winter warmer to be served with warm crusty bread and if you like, a slice of cheese.
Instead of canned baked beans, you can also use navy (haricot) beans, soaked overnight and then pressure cooked until they are soft. The addition of cream to the soup balances the acidic taste of the tomatoes. You can adjust the quantities to suit your palate. Always present a container of grated or shredded parmesan cheese (or processed cheese in case you cannot find it) to sprinkle into each soup bowl.

 Preparation time : 10 minutes. Cooking time : 15 minutes. Serves 4.

½ cup baked beans (canned)
1 medium onion, sliced
2 cloves garlic, sliced
1 cup tomatoes, chopped
¼ cup macaroni or any small pasta
2 teaspoons cornflour
1 teaspoon dried oregano
2 tablespoons cream
2 tablespoons tomato ketchup
2 tablespoons butter
salt and freshly ground pepper to taste

For the garnish
4 tablespoons grated parmesan cheese or
processed cheese

1. Heat the butter in a pan, add the onion and garlic and sauté till the onion turns translucent.
2. Add the baked beans, tomatoes, macaroni, salt and 4 cups of hot water and bring to a boil. Simmer till the macaroni is cooked (approx. 8 to 10 minutes).
3. Dissolve the cornflour in 2 tablespoons of water and add to the soup.
4. Add the oregano, cream, tomato ketchup and freshly ground pepper and mix well.
   Serve hot, garnished with the cheese.

BROCCOLI SOUP

Picture on page 26

*Italian cooking has all kinds of soups, "Minestra" being one of the kinds.
Minestra soups start with a light broth to which pasta or vegetables are added to give depth and a subtle flavour.
Crisp, crunchy vegetables, lightly thickened with pasta is what makes this soup delicious!
This soup is an ideal first course, a prelude to a heartier main course.*

 Preparation time : 10 minutes. Cooking time : 12 minutes. Serves 3 to 4.

1 cup broccoli, cut into small florets
½ cup onion, thinly sliced
1 large clove garlic, chopped
½ cup carrots, thinly sliced
2 tablespoons chopped celery
1 tablespoon alphabet pasta or stellini (or any small pasta)
¼ cup sun-dried tomatoes, page 142, soaked and thinly sliced
1 tablespoon olive oil or butter
salt and freshly ground pepper to taste

For serving
4 tablespoons grated parmesan cheese or processed cheese

1. Heat the olive oil in a pan, add the onion, garlic, carrots and celery and sauté for 2 to 3 minutes.
2. Add the broccoli, pasta, salt and 2½ cups of hot water and simmer till the pasta is cooked (approx. 5 to 7 minutes).
3. Add the sun-dried tomatoes and pepper and mix well.
   Serve hot with the parmesan cheese.

POTATO, PASTA & PESTO SOUP

For everyday living in Italy, the family's main meal often begins with bowls of hot "brodo" (broth).
The broth is lightly seasoned and may have a little pasta or bits of vegetables or it can be a thick, creamy and wholesome soup, sufficiently filling to make a meal. Lots of potatoes, carrots, milk and cheese gives this soup its unique velvety quality. Parsley and pesto lend it a delicate aromatic flavour. Pasta and potatoes both thicken the soup. So before serving, you may need to add a little water if the soup gets too thick.

 Preparation time : 10 minutes. Cooking time : 18 minutes. Serves 4.

1 cup potato, peeled and finely chopped
½ cup carrots, peeled and finely chopped
1 cup onions, finely chopped
2 cups milk
2 tablespoons macaroni or shell pasta
1 tablespoon parsley, finely chopped
2 tablespoons butter or olive oil
salt and pepper to taste

To be pounded into a pesto
12 to 14 basil leaves
2 or 3 walnut halves
1 large clove garlic, crushed
1 tablespoon olive oil or oil

For the garnish

4 tablespoons grated cheese

1. Heat the butter in a pan, add the potato, carrots and onions and sauté for about 3 to 4 minutes.
2. Add the milk, macaroni, 2 cups of hot water, salt and pepper and simmer for about 10 to 12 minutes until the pasta is cooked.
3. Just before serving, re-heat the soup, add the parsley, prepared pesto and mix well.
   Serve hot, topped with the cheese.

 HANDY TIP You can add 2 teaspoons of ready pesto instead of the paste mentioned above. Add the pesto and parsley just before you serve the soup as they will retain their colour.

BUTTER BEAN & VEGETABLE SOUP

White butter beans called cannelini (in Florence) are the traditional base for soups. These beans are cooked and used to quickly assemble flavourful and wholesome soups.

You can choose any combination of vegetables. This is a soup with the look of summer and is delightful when eaten with a loaf of garlic or crusty bread.

 Preparation time : 15 minutes. Cooking time : 25 minutes. Serves 4.

½ cup dried butter beans (lima beans or pavta)
½ cup onions, diced
2 stalks celery, sliced
1 large clove garlic, chopped
2 bay leaves
½ cup carrots, diced
½ cup cabbage, shredded
1½ cups tomatoes, chopped
4 tablespoons tomato purée
2 tablespoons cooked rice
2 tablespoons olive oil or oil
salt and freshly ground pepper to taste

1. Soak the butter beans overnight. Drain and keep aside.
2. Combine the beans with 2 cups of water and pressure cook till they are overdone. Drain the water and discard it.
3. Heat the olive oil and add the bay leaves, onions, celery and garlic and sauté till the onions are translucent.
4. Add the carrots, cabbage and salt and sauté for another 3 to 4 minutes.
5. Add the tomatoes, tomato purée, butter beans, rice and 4 cups of hot water.
6. Bring to a boil and simmer for 5 to 10 minutes till the carrots are soft.
7. Discard the bay leaves and finish with freshly ground pepper.
   Serve hot with crusty bread.

ROMAN STYLE PUMPKIN SOUP

A version of the classic Roman soup. Pumpkins and leeks are puréed together to get a creamy, velvety soup.
A dash of fresh mint adds that necessary flavour.
Pumpkins are usually large vegetables. To make things a little easier, ask your greengrocer to cut a chunk off for you. The addition of potato gives a little thickness to the soup, but you can omit it if you are an avid pumpkin lover!

 Preparation time : 5 minutes. Cooking time : 15 minutes. Serves 4.

2 cups red pumpkin (kaddu), peeled and cubed
½ cup potato, peeled and cut into cubes
½ cup spring onions, chopped
1 large clove garlic, chopped
1 cup milk
½ teaspoon dried thyme or mixed herbs
3 tablespoons butter or olive oil
salt and freshly ground pepper to taste

For the garnish

1 tablespoon mint, chopped

1. Melt the butter in a pan and sauté the spring onions and garlic for 1 minute.
2. Add the pumpkin and potato and sauté for about 3 minutes.
3. Add the milk and 1 cup of hot water, mix well and simmer on a slow flame till the potatoes are cooked.
4. Allow the mixture to cool completely and then purée in the blender.
5. Combine the puréed mixture and thyme with 2 cups of hot water in a pan.
6. Season with salt and pepper and bring to a boil.
   Serve hot, garnished with the mint.

SALADS

Salads are served as antipasto or as a separate course
by themselves. Use Italian staples such as extra virgin
olive oil and cheese. It really does contribute a lot to
the dish. Cook vegetables till they are "al dente" and
slightly crisp so that they retain their nutrients and the
colours remain bright. Create your own concoctions using
your favourite greens, pasta or beans in a
dressing of your choice.
It is important to remember to serve these salads at the
correct temperature, whether warm, chilled or at room
temperature as that can make or mar your salad.

NEAPOLITAN POTATO SALAD

Picture on page 26

The Neapolitan style of cooking is characterised by the famous piazzaiola sauce. It consists of peeled, chopped and deseeded tomatoes, garlic, basil or marjoram and olive oil. It is served with pasta, grilled dishes and pizzas.

Cooked potatoes with deseeded tomatoes, the Neapolitan way are a favourite Italian salad. This salad is like the one served in Naples which goes well as an accompaniment to a burger and is delicious just by itself.

Chill this salad thoroughly before serving!

 Preparation time : 10 minutes. Cooking time : 15 minutes. Serves 4.

3 to 4 medium potatoes
2 to 3 medium tomatoes
2 spring onions, sliced
½ cup grated mozzarella cheese or cooking cheese
4 to 6 stuffed green olives, sliced
1 tablespoon olive oil or oil
1 large clove garlic, chopped
6 to 8 basil leaves, chopped
salt and freshly ground pepper to taste

1. Boil the potatoes. Cut them into small cubes and chill thoroughly.
2. Slice each tomato into 2 portions vertically. Remove the seeds and pulp and discard it.
3. Cut the deseeded tomatoes into thin slices.
4. Combine all the ingredients in a large bowl and mix well.
5. Chill for at least an hour before serving so that the flavours blend well. Serve chilled.

PASTA SALAD WITH BASIL VINAIGRETTE

Sun-dried tomatoes and olives enhance this delicious pesto-inspired salad which is just as tasty whether served warm or cold.

When using pasta in a salad, it is important to rinse the cooked pasta with cold water and drain it well. Toss a little oil through the pasta to stop it from sticking together.

Elaborations of a pasta salad are many. You may add slivers of vegetables, a few herb leaves (particularly basil), or other refinements such as sun-drenched tomatoes or olives. Serve dressed with olive oil and lemon juice. So with a little imagination, you can create your own salad recipe!

 Preparation time : 20 minutes. No cooking. Serves 4.

1½ cups cooked fusilli, page 138
1 large tomato, blanched and peeled
2 tablespoons sun-dried tomatoes, page 142, soaked and finely chopped
8 to 10 black olives, deseeded
2 tablespoons chopped walnuts
4 tablespoons mozzarella cheese or cheese, thinly sliced

To be mixed together into the basil vinaigrette dressing
1 tablespoon chopped fresh basil leaves
1 clove garlic, finely chopped
1 tablespoon olive oil
1 tablespoon lemon juice
salt and freshly ground pepper to taste

1. Deseed the tomato and cut into thick strips.
2. Toss all the ingredients for the salad except the vinaigrette dressing.
   Chill the salad for at least 2 to 3 hours.
3. Just before serving, add the dressing to the salad. Mix well.
   Serve with garlic bread.

 HANDY TIP   If you are using sun-dried tomatoes preserved in
olive oil, you do not need to soak them in water.

THREE BEAN SALAD

Picture on page 111

Tuscans take great pride in cooking and eating and are known for their hefty appetites. Beans appear frequently in many guises in their cooking, as they are filling and form a substantial meal.

This Tuscan inspired salad is a combination of beans in an oregano tomato dressing which makes a quick and tasty salad.

The beans need to be soaked overnight and pressure cooked separately till they are soft. The ketchup used in the dressing lends a sweet and concentrated tomato flavour, which blends beautifully in the salad.

 Preparation time : 20 minutes. No cooking. Serves 4.

¼ cup boiled kidney beans (rajma)
½ cup boiled chick peas (kabuli chana)
½ cup boiled butter beans (lima beans or pavta)
2 spring onions, finely chopped
1 tomato, deseeded and cut into small cubes
¼ cup mozzarella cheese or cheese, cut into 12 mm. (½") cubes
1 cup iceberg lettuce, torn into pieces

To be mixed into a dressing
1½ tablespoons tomato ketchup
3 tablespoons olive oil or oil
¼ teaspoon dried oregano
salt and freshly ground pepper to taste

1. Combine all the ingredients except the dressing in a salad bowl. Toss well. Chill for at least 2 to 3 hours.
2. Just before serving, toss the dressing in the salad. Mix well. Serve immediately.

AVOCADO, TOMATO & MOZZARELLA PASTA SALAD

A stylish summer salad made from ingredients representing the three colours of the Italian flag - a sunny cheerful dish!

For Italians, the time of the year is important in determining which salad will be served. Vegetables, roots, pulses and herbs are always chosen when they are in season and at the peak of their perfection.

The avocado chosen for this salad should be ripe, so that it gives under the pressure of your finger and the seed within is loosened from its surrounding flesh. Halve the avocado, remove the stone and peel off the skin. Slice the flesh lengthwise. Apply a little lemon juice to the cut slices as they get discoloured on exposure to the air.

Add the dressing to this salad, cover and chill for at least 2 hours. You may need to add additional dressing if the salad appears too dry while serving.

 Preparation time : 10 minutes. No cooking. Serves 3 to 4.

1 ripe avocado, cut into thin slices
1 teaspoon lemon juice
3 large tomatoes, cut into thin slices
1½ cups cooked fusilli or bow pasta, page 138
1 cup mozzarella cheese, cut into thin slices
2 tablespoons chopped walnuts

To be mixed into a dressing
3 tablespoons olive oil or oil
1½ tablespoons lemon juice
¼ teaspoon mustard powder
2 tablespoons chopped fresh basil
¼ teaspoon sugar
salt and freshly ground pepper to taste

1. Apply the lemon juice to the avocado slices to prevent them from discoloring.

2. Combine all the ingredients of the salad in a serving bowl, add the dressing and toss well.
3. Cover and refrigerate for about 2 hours.
   Serve chilled.

PEACH LETTUCE SALAD

Picture on page 85

For a sophisticated start to an elaborate meal, try this simple salad of sweet canned peaches, mozzarella cubes, aromatic leaves of basil tossed with crispy lettuce. Peaches and lettuce blend well as salad mates. Fresh seasonal fruits like oranges, mangoes, pears can also be used.
Crispy greens with a dressing of a good olive oil made tart with fresh lemon juice is the basis for most delicious salads!

 Preparation time : 10 minutes. No cooking.   Serves 4.

2 cups lettuce (iceberg, Cos lettuce etc.), torn into pieces
1 cup peach, cut into cubes (canned)
½ cup mozzarella cheese, cubed
10 to 15 fresh basil leaves, torn into pieces
1 to 2 herbed pizza strips, page 21, cut into pieces (optional)

To be mixed into a dressing
2 tablespoons olive oil
1 tablespoon lemon juice
salt and freshly ground pepper to taste

1. Mix all the ingredients for the salad except the dressing in a serving bowl.
   Keep refrigerated.
2. Just before serving, add the dressing to the salad and toss well.
   Serve chilled.

HANDY TIPS 1. To keep the lettuce crisp, soak it in iced water for 10 to 15 minutes and then drain it thoroughly before using in the salad.
2. Drain out all the syrup from the peach halves before using them for the salad.

PIZZAS AND BREADS

The word "pizza" actually means a kind of "pie".
Pizzas originated in the old Italian city of
Naples as a street snack which was richly flavoured
and quickly made. It was not round and flat as we
know it today, but was folded up like a book with the
filling inside. Today pizzas are made with every
imaginable type of topping.
Flat breads are very popular in Italy.
They are called focaccias flavoured with herbs,
spices and cheese. Focaccia can be served as an
appetizer or as an accompaniment & even used as a
pizza base or filled like a sandwich.
Choose the best quality vegetables and herbs
for maximum flavour. It may seem complicated
to make a pizza or a bread at home for the first time,
but it will get easier as you get more familiar.
Nothing can quite compare with a home-made pizza
base and a freshly made tomato sauce.

PIZZA MARGHERITA

A classic pizza, named after the Italian Queen Margherita. On a visit to Naples, Queen Margherita requested for a local specialty. She was served a pizza in the colours of the Italian flag — red tomatoes, green basil and white mozzarella. The Queen was delighted and the dish was christened after her. If you cannot find fresh basil, substitute it with ½ teaspoon dried basil.

 Preparation time : 10 minutes. Cooking time : 40 minutes. Makes 2 pizzas.

1 recipe basic pizza base, page 134
1 recipe pizza sauce, page 139
10 to 12 fresh basil leaves, roughly chopped
1 cup cooking cheese or mozzarella cheese, grated
2 tablespoons olive oil
butter or oil for greasing

1. Place one pizza base on a greased baking tray.
2. Spread half the pizza sauce on the pizza base.
3. Sprinkle with half the basil leaves and cheese on top of the pizza.
4. Drizzle with half of the olive oil and bake in a pre-heated oven at 200°C (400°F) for 20 minutes or until the base is evenly browned.
5. Repeat with the remaining ingredients to make another pizza. Serve hot.

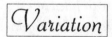
Variation

SKILLET MARGHERITA

Cook the pizza in a non-stick pan instead of baking it in the oven. Cover the pan with a lid and cook on a very slow flame for 10 to 12 minutes or till the base is evenly browned. The trick in making this pizza is to keep the flame sufficiently low so that the base does not burn while cooking.
You can follow this method of cooking for any regular crust pizza.

MUSHROOM & PEPPER PIZZA

Picture on page 51

Pizza bakers in Naples are often cooks, artists and actors, all in one. They can be seen through the windows of Pizzerias pulling, stretching and kneading the pizza dough, then spreading and sprinkling the topping over. The pizza tray is then pushed into the oven and the pizza baker starts his show all over again. Pizzas can be made very easily at home using conventional ovens.
I have topped the pizza with sautéed peppers and mushrooms. The base used here is an innovative polenta or cornmeal base. The choice of toppings is endless and can be varied according to the ingredients which happen to be on hand. Remember to always pre-heat the oven before putting the pizza in and to serve straight from the oven.

 Preparation time : 15 minutes. Cooking time : 40 minutes. Makes 2 pizzas.

1 recipe polenta pizza base, page 136

For the topping
½ cup mushrooms, sliced
½ green pepper, sliced
½ red pepper, sliced
½ yellow pepper, sliced
3 to 4 tablespoons olive oil or oil
salt to taste

Other ingredients
1 recipe pizza sauce, page 139
1 cup mozzarella cheese or cooking cheese, grated
1 teaspoon olive oil or oil
salt to taste

For the topping
1. Heat 1 tablespoon of olive oil and sauté the mushrooms till they are soft. Add salt and keep aside.

2. In the same manner, sauté all three coloured peppers in olive oil separately with a little salt till they are lightly caramelized. Keep aside.

How to proceed

1. Make the polenta pizza base as mentioned in the recipe.
2. Place one polenta pizza base on a greased baking tray.
3. Spread half the pizza sauce on the pizza base.
4. Arrange half of the mushrooms and peppers, one on each quarter of the pizza base as shown in the picture on facing page.
5. Sprinkle half of the grated cheese on top.
6. Bake in a pre-heated oven at 200°C (400°F) for 15 to 20 minutes or until the base is evenly browned.
7. Repeat with the remaining ingredients to make one more pizza.
   Serve hot.

1. **Risotto Fiorentina,** *page 103*
2. **Mushroom & Pepper Pizza,** *page 49*

PESTO PIZZA SANDWICH

Picture on facing page

This fun sandwich uses Italian bread (a herb flavoured bread) topped with a zesty salad bound with a pesto flavoured mayonnaise dressing.
If you are making pesto by hand, it is best to use a mortar and pestle. But you can make larger quantities in a blender and refrigerate it for upto a week.
Chill all the ingredients for the salad and combine them with the dressing just before serving.
You can choose your own vegetable combination for the salad.

 Preparation time : 15 minutes. Cooking time : 20 minutes. Makes 2 pizza sandwiches.

For the herb pizza base
1 cup whole wheat flour (gehun ka atta)
1 teaspoon (5 grams) fresh yeast, crumbled
½ teaspoon sugar
2 tablespoons onion, finely chopped
½ teaspoon dried thyme
½ teaspoon dried oregano
1 tablespoon olive oil or oil
½ teaspoon salt
oil for greasing

To be mixed into a topping
1 cup iceberg lettuce, torn into pieces
½ cup baby corn, diced and blanched
1 tablespoon sweet corn kernels, boiled

1. **Spaghetti with Eggplant Parmagianna,** *page 79*
2. **Pesto Pizza Sandwhich,** *recipe above*

2 to 3 cherry tomatoes (optional)
2 tablespoons mozzarella cheese, cubed
1 tablespoon sun-dried tomatoes, page 142, soaked and finely chopped
2 tablespoons finely chopped celery

To be mixed into a dressing
1 tablespoon pesto, page 140
2 tablespoons eggless mayonnaise, page 144
salt and pepper to taste

For serving
grated parmesan cheese

For the herb pizza base
1. Combine all the ingredients except the olive oil in a bowl and knead into a soft dough using enough water until it is smooth and elastic (approx. 5 to 7 minutes).
2. Add the olive oil and knead again.
3. Cover the dough with a wet muslin cloth and allow it to prove till it doubles in volume (approx. 15 to 20 minutes).
4. Press the dough lightly to remove the air. Divide the dough into 2 equal parts.
5. Roll out each portion of the dough into an oval that is approx. 6 mm. (¼") thick and about 150 mm. (6") long. Prick with a fork at regular intervals.
7. Place the oval pizza bases on a greased baking tray.
8. Bake in a pre-heated oven at 200°C (400°F) for 10 minutes or until the base is evenly browned. Allow it to cool.

How to proceed
1. Just before serving, toss the greens and vegetables in the dressing mixture.
2. Put this salad on top of the pizza bases. Sprinkle on top with the parmesan cheese.
3. Cut into wedges and serve immediately.

 HANDY TIP   Refrigerate all the ingredients for the topping and mix the pesto and mayonnaise just before serving.

BROCCOLI PIZZA PIE

Filled breads are the most appealing. They are great for buffet presentations and have the element of surprise when the contents are revealed.

Rustic pizza pies come from rural Southern Italy. Unlike pizzas which cooked quickly at a high temperature, they are baked at a moderate heat to allow the ingredients inside to cook evenly.

The broccoli can be substituted using any vegetable such as cauliflower or a combination of garden fresh veggies!

 Preparation time : 15 minutes. Cooking time : 25 minutes. Makes 1 pizza pie.

½ recipe basic pizza base, page 134
4 tablespoons pizza sauce, page 139
butter or oil for greasing

For the filling
1½ cups broccoli, finely chopped
⅓ cup onions, chopped
1 tablespoon garlic, chopped
¼ teaspoon dried mixed herbs
1½ cups cooking cheese or mozzarella cheese, grated
1 tablespoon butter
salt and pepper to taste

For glazing
2 tablespoons milk
1 tablespoon butter

For the filling
1. Heat the butter in a pan, add the onions and garlic and sauté till the onions turn translucent.
2. Add the broccoli and sauté for 2 to 3 minutes.
3. Cool the mixture, add the mixed herbs, cheese, salt and pepper and mix well. Keep aside.

How to proceed

1. Roll out ⅔ of the dough into a 200 mm. (8") diameter circle and the other ⅓ portion into a 150 mm. (6") diameter circle.
2. Line the base and sides of a greased 150 mm. (6") diameter pie dish with the larger (⅔) portion of the rolled dough.
3. Spread the pizza sauce on the base.
4. Add the filling and cover with the smaller portion of the rolled dough.
5. Seal the edges using a little water and trim the edges using a knife. Discard the excess dough. Prick the top of the pie with a fork at regular intervals.
6. Brush the top with the milk.
7. Bake in a pre-heated oven at 180°C (360°F) for about 20 minutes or till evenly browned.
8. Remove from the oven and glaze with the butter.
9. Cut into wedges and serve hot.

WHOLESOME DEEP DISH PIZZA

Thick crusty pizza bread topped with a delicious mix of vegetable textures, surprising flavours and colourful appearance.
This pizza is baked in a deep pie dish or a deep dish. Experiment with your own topping ideas and combinations.

 Preparation time : 15 minutes. Cooking time : 25 minutes. Makes 1 pizza.

½ recipe basic pizza base, page 134
½ recipe pizza sauce, page 139
butter or oil for greasing

To be mixed into a topping

1½ cups mixed vegetables (baby corn, spring onions, olives, capsicum, mushrooms), sliced
2 teaspoons chilli flakes
2 tablespoons fresh basil, chopped
salt to taste

For baking

½ cup cooking cheese or mozzarella cheese, grated
1 tablespoon olive oil or oil

1. Roll out the pizza dough into a circle of 200 mm. (8") diameter and 8 mm. (⅓") thickness. Line a 150 mm. (6") greased pie dish with it.
2. Spread the pizza sauce over the base and fill with the topping.
3. Top with the cheese and finally drizzle the olive oil over it.
4. Bake in a pre-heated oven at 180°C (360°F) for about 20 minutes or until the base is evenly browned.
   Serve hot.

FOUR CHEESE PIZZA

For Italians, a pizza is an extension of bread. Pizza in some form has always been present throughout most of Italian history and every region has its own favourite recipe.

Whole wheat pizza topped with sautéed leeks and four cheese flavours is a classic recipe. You can use any variety of cheese you like.

An array of flavoured cheeses is available at gourmet stores like herb-flavoured cheese, paprika cheese, pepper cheese, garlic cheese. These can be made at home by mixing the desired flavouring ingredients like pepper, garlic etc. with mozzarella or cooking cheese. Flavoured cheese spreads can also be used.

 Preparation time : 15 minutes. Cooking time : 40 minutes. Makes 2 pizzas.

1 recipe wholemeal pizza base, page 135
1 recipe pizza sauce, page 139
butter or oil for greasing

For the topping

2 cups leeks or spring onions, chopped
3 cloves garlic, chopped
a pinch of nutmeg (jaiphal)
1 tablespoon butter or oil
salt to taste

For baking

¼ cup pepper cheese, grated
¼ cup garlic cheese, grated
¼ cup paprika cheese, grated
¼ cup mozzarella cheese or cooking cheese, grated

For the topping

1. Heat the butter in a pan.
2. Add the leeks, garlic, nutmeg and salt and stir-fry for 3 to 4 minutes.
   Keep aside.

How to proceed

1. Place one pizza base on a greased baking tray.
2. Spread half the pizza sauce and half the topping on it.
3. Divide each of the cheeses into 2 equal portions and place them on the pizza
   in such a way that each type of cheese occupies one quarter of the pizza.
4. Bake in a pre-heated oven at 200°C (400°F) for 15 to 20 minutes
   or till the base is evenly browned.
5. Repeat with the remaining ingredients to make another pizza.
   Serve hot.

PIZZA GARDENIA

A thin crust pizza topped with pesto and a colourful combination of fresh vegetables. Italians use only freshly picked seasonal vegetables when they are at the height of perfection. They rarely let any vegetable grow past its prime.

 Preparation time : 15 minutes. Cooking time : 50 minutes. Makes 2 pizzas.

1 recipe basic pizza base, page 134
1 recipe pesto, page 140

For the roasted vegetable topping

1 medium red pepper, sliced
1 medium green pepper, sliced
1 zucchini, sliced
1 onion, sliced
1 eggplant (baingan), sliced

1 clove garlic, chopped
1 teaspoon butter
1 tablespoon olive oil or oil
salt and pepper to taste

Other ingredients
1 cup mozzarella cheese or cooking cheese, grated
butter or oil for greasing

For the roasted vegetable topping
Heat the butter and olive oil in a pan, add all the remaining ingredients and
cook over a high flame, stirring continuously till the vegetables are slightly
browned. Remove and keep aside.

How to proceed
1. Place one pizza base on a greased baking tray.
2. Spread half of the pesto on top of the pizza base.
3. Top with half of the roasted vegetables and mozzarella cheese.
4. Bake in a pre-heated oven at 200°C (400°F) for 15 to 20 minutes or till the
   base is evenly browned.
5. Repeat with the remaining ingredients to make one more pizza.
   Serve hot.

SPINACH & RICOTTA PIE

*The Italian word "pizza" simply means a "pie" and although they are not
conventional pies in the strict sense of the word, there are some classic versions of
pizzas which are pies with double crusts.
They are baked in large tins and then sliced for serving.
Spinach and ricotta pie is a classic pizza pie, a whole meal pizza pie enclosing a
filling of garlic, spinach, ricotta cheese, cheese and sultanas, baked and served warm.
You can make this recipe ahead of time and re-heat it just before serving.*

 Preparation time : 30 minutes. Cooking time : 30 minutes. Serves 4.

For the crust
1 recipe wholemeal pizza base, page 135
butter or oil for greasing

For the filling
2 cups spinach, finely chopped
½ cup ricotta cheese or paneer (cottage cheese), crumbled
¼ cup onion, chopped
2 cloves garlic, chopped
1 tablespoon sultanas
½ cup cheese, grated
a pinch of nutmeg (jaiphal)
1 tablespoon olive oil or oil
salt and pepper to taste

For glazing
2 tablespoons milk
1 tablespoon butter

For the filling
1. Heat the olive oil in a pan and sauté the onion till it turns translucent.
2. Add the garlic and sauté for one minute.
3. Add the spinach and sauté for a further 5 minutes.
4. Add the ricotta cheese, sultanas and cheese and mix well. Season with salt, pepper and nutmeg.
5. Keep aside.

How to proceed
1. Roll out ⅔ of the dough into a 200 mm. (8") diameter circle and the other ⅓ portion into a 150 mm. (6") diameter circle.
2. Line the base and sides of a greased 150 mm. (6") diameter pie dish with the larger (⅔) portion of the rolled dough.
3. Spread the filling and cover with the smaller rolled dough.
4. Seal the edges using a little water and trim the edges using a knife. Discard the excess dough. Prick the top of the pie with a fork at regular intervals.
5. Brush the top with the milk.
6. Bake in a pre-heated oven at 180°C (360°F) for about 20 minutes or till evenly browned.
7. Remove from the oven and glaze with the butter.
8. Cut into wedges and serve hot.

ROMAN STYLE PIZZA WITH MUSHROOMS, GARLIC & WALNUTS

When wandering the streets of Rome, it is hard to miss the displays of big, succulent slabs of pizzas in the windows of pizzerias.
Individual servings are cut off as ordered. Businessmen, school children and tourists alike all queue up throughout the day for the most inviting of snacks— the pizza.
Toppings are deceptively simple using a few ingredients. This recipe is of a delectable whole wheat pizza topped with mushrooms, garlic and walnuts, flavoured with lots of fresh and dried herbs!

 Preparation time : 15 minutes. Cooking time : 40 minutes. Makes 2 pizzas.

1 recipe wholemeal pizza base, page 135
1 recipe pizza sauce, page 139
butter or oil for greasing

For the topping
1 cup cooking cheese or mozzarella cheese, grated
1 teaspoon dried mixed herbs
2 teaspoons chilli flakes
1 cup fresh mushrooms, thickly sliced
1 teaspoon garlic, finely chopped
⅓ cup walnuts, chopped
¼ cup fresh basil leaves, chopped
salt to taste

1. Mix together the cheese, mixed herbs and chilli flakes. Keep aside.
2. Place one pizza base on a greased baking tray.
3. Spread half the pizza sauce over the pizza base.
4. Arrange half of the mushrooms, garlic, walnuts and basil leaves and sprinkle some salt on top.
5. Top with half the quantity of the prepared cheese mixture.

6. Bake in a pre-heated oven at 200°C (400°F) for 15 to 20 minutes or until the base is evenly browned.
7. Repeat for the other pizza base and the remaining ingredients. Serve hot.

CALZONE

A calzone is like a folded over stuffed pizza. The circle of pizza dough is folded in half over the filling and then sealed. During baking, the pizza dough swells somewhat until it resembles a "stuffed stocking", the literal translation of word calzone.

Sautéed vegetables and cheese aromatized with herbs is the filling for this calzone. You can vary the vegetable combination if you like.

For a change, try frying the calzone until golden brown in hot oil. You will find that it is easier to handle the calzone during frying when it has been formed into appetiser sized Calzonetti (or smaller calzones). Calzone can stand alone as a substantial snack or combined with a green salad and soup, it makes an easy dinner.

 Preparation time : 20 minutes. Cooking time : 30 minutes. Makes 4.

½ recipe basic pizza base, page 134
butter or oil for greasing and glazing

For the filling
½ cup mushrooms, sliced
1 red pepper, sliced
1 onion, sliced
1 large clove garlic, chopped
1 teaspoon plain flour (maida)
¼ cup milk
1 tablespoon cheese, grated
1 teaspoon dried oregano
1 tablespoon butter
salt to taste

For the filling

1. Heat the butter in a saucepan and sauté the onion and garlic for one minute.
2. Add the mushrooms and red pepper and sauté for some more time.
3. Sprinkle the flour and add the milk, cheese, oregano and salt and mix well. Bring it to a boil.
4. Divide the mixture into 4 portions. Allow it to cool. Keep aside.

How to proceed

1. Divide the pizza dough into 4 equal portions. Keep aside under a wet cloth.
2. Roll out each portion of the dough into a 150 mm. (6") diameter circle.
3. Put one portion of the filling on each circle.
4. Fold each circle to form a semicircle.
5. Seal the ends using a little water and press the edges firmly with the help of a fork.
6. Place on a greased baking tray. Cover with a wet cloth and keep for 10 minutes or until it doubles in volume.
7. Bake in a pre-heated oven at 200°C (400°F) for about 15 minutes or until they are evenly browned.
8. Remove from the oven and brush with melted butter. Serve hot.

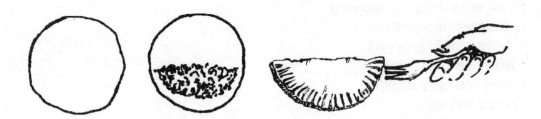

ONION & THYME FOCACCIA

Named from "focus", the Latin for hearth, focaccia were baked by housewives on heated hearth stones before the oven became commonplace. They originated in Liguria, Italy and have always been flavoured simply but with ingredients of the best quality.

Focaccias or flat breads have changed little over the centuries and the invention of the oven is the only modernisation they have undergone.

This is a traditional recipe made using yeast. Try serving wedges of this fresh focaccia with the olive cream cheese dip, page 27.

 Preparation time : 15 minutes. Cooking time : 15 minutes. Serves 3 to 4.

For the dough
1 cup plain flour (maida)
1 teaspoon (5 grams) fresh yeast, crumbled
½ teaspoon sugar
1 tablespoon olive oil or oil
½ teaspoon salt

To be mixed into a topping
½ teaspoon dried thyme
½ onion, finely chopped
1 teaspoon chilli flakes
1 teaspoon olive oil or oil
½ teaspoon salt

Other ingredients
olive oil or oil for greasing and glazing

1. Combine all the ingredients for the dough, except the olive oil, in a bowl and knead into a soft dough using enough water until it is smooth and elastic (approx. 5 to 7 minutes).
2. Add the olive oil and knead again.
3. Cover the dough with a wet muslin cloth and allow it to prove till it doubles in volume (approx. 15 to 20 minutes).

4. Press the dough lightly to remove the air.
5. Roll out the dough into a circle of 250 mm. (10") diameter and 6 mm. (¼") thickness.
6. Place the dough on a greased baking tray and spread the topping mixture onto it. Prick with a fork at regular intervals.
7. Bake in a pre-heated oven at 220°C (430°F) for 10 to 12 minutes or until the focaccia is golden brown.
8. Remove from the oven and brush with olive oil.
   Serve hot, cut into wedges.

SMOKED PEPPER & CHEESE BREAD

This wholesome Milanese bread is ideal for a country picnic. And is also equally good for a buffet presentation.
Smoked pepper and cheese bread is essentially a layered pizza bread sandwich baked in a round tin. Serve it hot, warm, cold or reheated. Hearty soups or salads are ideal companions.

 Preparation time : 20 minutes. Cooking time : 50 minutes. Serves 4 to 6.

1 recipe basic pizza base, page 134

For the filling mixture
1 medium red pepper
1 medium green pepper
1 medium yellow pepper
½ cup grated cheese
½ teaspoon dried rosemary
salt to taste

Other ingredients
oil for greasing and glazing

For the filling mixture
1. Grill the red, green and yellow pepper in a pre-heated oven at 200°C (400°F) for 10 to 15 minutes till the skin is dark brown.

2. Allow it to cool and peel the skin off.
3. Cut into small pieces and combine with the cheese, rosemary and salt. Mix well.

How to proceed
1. Divide the pizza dough into 3 equal parts.
2. Roll out each portion of the dough into a circle of 125 mm. (5") diameter.
3. Place one circle in a greased tin of 125 mm. (5") diameter.
4. Top with half of the pepper and cheese filling mixture.
5. Place another circle of the rolled dough. Press firmly at the ends so as to seal the filling inside the two dough circles.
6. Top with the remaining pepper and cheese filling mixture.
7. Cover with the third dough circle and seal the ends tightly. Allow it to prove under a wet muslin cloth for 10 minutes or till it doubles in volume. Prick with a fork at regular intervals.
8. Bake in a pre-heated oven at 180°C (360°F) for 30 to 35 minutes or until golden brown and the bread sounds hollow when tapped.
9. Unmould and allow to cool slightly. Brush with oil, cut into wedges and serve warm.

SUN-DRIED TOMATO LOAF

The end result here really justifies the extra effort required for making home-made bread. The yeasty flavours of the bread complements that of the chewy sun-dried tomatoes and basil.
You can also make mini sun-dried tomato rolls for children. Divide the dough into 8 equal portions, leave to rise and bake at 200°C (400°F) for 10 to 20 minutes.

 Preparation time : 50 minutes. Cooking time : 25 minutes. Makes 1 loaf.

1 cup whole wheat flour (gehun ka atta)
1 cup plain flour (maida)
2 teaspoons (10 grams) fresh yeast, crumbled
1 teaspoon salt
1 teaspoon sugar

2 tablespoons olive oil or oil

¼ cup sun-dried tomatoes, page 142, soaked and chopped

1 tablespoon chopped fresh basil

1 tablespoon tomato purée

oil or butter for greasing and glazing

1. Combine both the flours, yeast, salt and sugar and knead into a soft dough using enough water until it is smooth and elastic (approx. 5 to 7 minutes).
2. Add the olive oil and knead again.
3. Allow it to prove under a wet muslin cloth till it doubles in volume (approx. 15 to 20 minutes).
4. Press the dough lightly to remove the air.
5. Add the sun-dried tomatoes, basil and tomato purée and knead again, adding some more flour if required.
6. Roll the dough out into a square of 200 mm. x 200 mm. (8" x 8").
7. Roll it up like a Swiss roll, sealing the edges by pinching the dough tightly.
8. Place on a greased baking tray with the sealed side facing downwards.
9. Cover with a wet muslin cloth and allow it to prove till it doubles in volume (approx. 15 to 20 minutes).
10. Bake in a pre-heated oven at 180°C (360°F) for 20 to 25 minutes or until the loaf springs back when touched. Remove from the oven and brush with oil.
11. Allow it to cool. Cut into slices and serve.

STUFFED FOCACCIA

This Italian flat bread has got its name from the Latin word focus, which means "hearth". Italian style ingredients such as roasted peppers, sun-dried tomatoes, olives, fragrant fresh or firm ripe tomatoes will complement this bread dough to perfection.

I have used a combination of cottage cheese (paneer) and cubes of mozzarella that melts just perfectly inside the focaccia.

Focaccia is very similar to a pizza base but this recipe uses two pizza bases sandwiched with a cheese and basil mixture.

Sea salt sprinkled on top of the focaccia gives it a delicious crust.

Bake this bread just before dinner and enjoy it with a bowl of hot soup.

1 recipe basic pizza base, page 134
½ cup cottage cheese (paneer), crumbled
½ cup cooking cheese or mozzarella cheese, cut into small cubes
10 to 15 basil leaves, torn into pieces
1 teaspoon chilli flakes
salt to taste

Other ingredients
½ teaspoon sea salt (khada namak)
butter or oil for greasing and brushing

1. Prepare the pizza dough as mentioned in the recipe. Divide the dough into 2 equal parts.
2. Roll out each portion into a circle of 200 mm. (8") diameter and 8 mm. (⅓") thickness.
3. Place one dough circle on a 200 mm. (8") greased pie dish.
4. Top with the cottage cheese, cheese, basil leaves, chilli flakes and salt.
5. Top with the second dough circle and seal the ends tightly, using a little water.
6. Brush the top of the focaccia with a little water and sprinkle the sea salt over. Prick the focaccia with a fork at regular intervals.
7. Bake in a pre-heated oven at 220°C (430°F) for 15 to 20 minutes or until the base is evenly browned.
8. Brush the hot focaccia with butter.
   Serve warm, cut into wedges.

HOME-MADE PASTA

Fettuccine, tagliatelle, ravioli, tortellini are some of the many pasta favourites that can be made at home. Traditionally, fresh pasta dough is made using flour, eggs and olive oil but all of the recipes have been tested without the use of eggs and they taste just as good. You can add fresh herbs to the dough or fill the pasta sheets with a filling of your choice. Or simply make fettuccine and then toss it with a lip smacking sauce of your choice. You can enrich these pasta doughs by adding vegetable purées of spinach, beet, and carrot. They will look more colourful too. It is essential that the pasta sheets be rolled out as thinly as you can manage. They should be almost translucent. Care should be taken not to tear the sheets. Use cornflour to dust while rolling out the dough as it makes rolling easier.

GREEN TAGLIATELLE WITH MUSHROOMS & BROCCOLI

Picture on page 86

Tagliatelle is a flat ribbon pasta which is native to Naples, the home of pasta dishes. Spinach tagliatelle tossed in mustard and brandy flavoured cheese sauce with the freshness of mushrooms and broccoli is simply marvellous. The addition of cheese spread to the sauce makes it of good thick coating consistency.
Like the city of Naples, this sauce is mellow and sophisticated.
This sauce also works well using plain fettuccine or spaghetti.

 Preparation time : 15 minutes. Cooking time : 30 minutes. Serves 4.

For the green tagliatelle
1 recipe spinach (vegetable) pasta dough, page 138
1 teaspoon salt and 1 tablespoon oil for cooking the pasta

For the mushroom and broccoli sauce
2 cups mushrooms, sliced
1 cup broccoli, cut into small florets
2 cloves garlic, finely chopped
2 cups milk
½ cup cheese spread
½ teaspoon french style mustard
4 tablespoons brandy (optional)
1 tablespoon finely chopped parsley
1 tablespoon olive oil or oil
salt and pepper to taste

For the green tagliatelle
1. Divide the pasta dough into 2 portions and roll out each portion as thinly as possible.
2. Cut each pasta sheet into a 250 mm. x 250 mm. (10" x 10") square.
3. Dust the pasta sheet with plenty of flour and roll it up like a Swiss roll. Cut into 6 mm. (¼") strips.

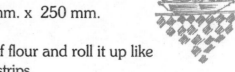

4. Heat plenty of water in a broad pan and add 1 teaspoon of salt and 1 tablespoon of oil. Add a few strands of the tagliatelle to the boiling water at a time and cook for 2 minutes.
5. Drain and transfer to a bowl of cold water to refresh it. Drain again and keep aside.

For the mushroom and broccoli sauce
1. Heat the olive oil in a pan, add the garlic and sauté for a few seconds.
2. Add the mushrooms and broccoli and sauté for 2 minutes.
3. Add the milk, cheese spread, mustard, salt and pepper and mix well. Bring to a boil, while stirring continuously.
4. Add the brandy and parsley and mix well. Keep aside.
5. Just before serving, reheat the sauce and toss the green tagliatelle in it. Serve hot.

CANNELLONI (CLASSIC)

The word cannelloni is derived from 'canna' and literally means big tubes of pasta. Pasta sheets are cooked, filled and rolled up into a cylindrical shape to form cannelloni.

This recipe is a lighter alternative to the cheese and calorie laden traditional recipe. Filled with baby corn, mushrooms, spinach and olives, the cannelloni is coated with a creamy white sauce.

You can buy ready cannelloni sheets instead of making it at home.

Serve this recipe with garlic bread and a tossed green salad.

 Preparation time : 30 minutes. Cooking time : 35 minutes. Serves 4.

For the cannelloni
1 recipe fresh pasta dough, page 137
1 teaspoon salt and 1 tablespoon oil for cooking the pasta

For the filling
1 cup mushrooms, sliced
1 cup baby corn, sliced

1 cup spinach, blanched, drained and finely chopped
6 to 8 stuffed green olives, sliced
1 teaspoon chopped garlic
2 spring onions, finely chopped
1 teaspoon dried oregano
3 tablespoons grated cheese
1 tablespoon cream
1 tablespoon butter
salt and pepper to taste

For the white sauce
2 tablespoons butter
1 tablespoon plain flour (maida)
1½ cups milk
salt and pepper to taste

Other ingredients
2 tablespoons grated cheese
butter or oil for greasing

For the cannelloni
1. Prepare the pasta dough as mentioned in the recipe.
2. Divide the pasta dough into 6 portions and roll out each portion as thinly as possible.
3. Cut each portion of the rolled out dough into a 100 mm. x 150 mm. (4" x 6") rectangle to make 6 cannelloni sheets.
4. Boil plenty of water in a broad pan and add 1 teaspoon of salt and 1 tablespoon of oil.
5. Drop the prepared pasta one sheet at a time into the boiling water and cook each sheet for 2 minutes.
6. Drain and transfer into a bowl of cold water to refresh it. Drain again and keep aside.

For the filling
1. Heat the butter in a pan, add the garlic, spring onions, Mushrooms and baby corn and sauté for 3 to 4 minutes.

2. Add the spinach, stuffed olives, oregano, cheese, cream, salt and pepper and mix well. Keep aside.

For the white sauce
1. Heat the butter, add the flour and sauté for 1 minute.
2. Slowly pour in the milk, whisking it continuously so that no lumps form. Bring to a boil.
3. Add salt and pepper and mix well. Remove from the fire.

How to proceed
1. Place one cooked pasta sheet on a dry surface.
2. Spread 2 tablespoons of the filling mixture on one side of the sheet. Roll up the pasta sheet tightly.
3. Repeat for the remaining pasta sheets.
4. Place all the prepared cannelloni on a greased baking dish.
5. Spoon the white sauce over the cannelloni.
6. Sprinkle the cheese on top and bake in a pre-heated oven at 220°C (430°F) for 10 to 15 minutes.
   Serve hot.

ZUCCHINI & EGGPLANT LASAGNE

This elegant vegetable lasagne showcases both tomato and cheese sauces as well as a colourful layer of zucchini and eggplant slices.

This rich baked dish is packed with layers of pasta filled with vegetables and tomatoes, topped with Italian mozzarella cheese and baked until golden brown. Choose firm long slender eggplants which have lots of flavour and very few seeds. For a quick variation, you can buy ready dry pasta sheets (available at certain speciality stores) instead of freshly made pasta.

This recipe can be prepared upto 24 hours in advance and kept in the refrigerator until needed. A great dish for entertaining!

 Preparation time : 20 minutes. Cooking time : 1 hour Serves 4 to 6.

For the lasagne

1 recipe fresh whole wheat pasta dough, page 137
1 teaspoon salt and 1 tablespoon oil for cooking the pasta

For the tomato sauce

4 tomatoes, diced
1 large onion, chopped
1 large clove garlic, grated
1 stalk celery, chopped
1 tablespoon tomato ketchup
½ teaspoon dried oregano
1 tablespoon olive oil or oil
salt and pepper to taste

For the filling

2 to 3 large eggplants (baingan), thinly sliced
2 zucchinis, thinly sliced
2 teaspoons chopped garlic
2 teaspoons chopped parsley
2 tablespoons olive oil or oil
salt and pepper to taste

For the white sauce

1 tablespoon butter
1 tablespoon plain flour (maida)
1 cup milk
2 tablespoons grated cheese
salt and pepper to taste

For baking

2 tablespoons cheese, grated

For the lasagne

1. Divide the pasta dough into 3 equal portions and roll
   out each portion as thinly as possible into a circle of
   150 mm. (6") diameter lasagne sheet.

2. Cook each sheet of pasta (one at a time for 2 minutes) in a large pan of boiling water to which 1 teaspoon of salt and 1 tablespoon of oil has been added.
3. Drain and transfer the lasange sheets in a bowl of cold water.
4. Drain again and keep aside.

For the tomato sauce
1. Heat the oil in a pan, add the onion, garlic and celery and sauté for 3 to 4 minutes.
2. Add the tomatoes, salt and pepper and sauté for 4 to 5 minutes.
3. Add the tomato ketchup and oregano and mix well. Keep aside.

For the filling
1. Heat 1 teaspoon of the olive oil in a pan, add the garlic and parsley and remove from the fire. Drain the garlic and parsley and keep aside.
2. In another pan, heat 1 tablespoon of the olive oil and sauté the zucchini slices with salt till they are lightly browned. Keep aside.
3. Heat the remaining olive oil in a pan and cook the eggplant slices on both sides till they are lightly browned.
4. Sprinkle a little salt and keep aside.

For the white sauce
1. Heat the butter, add the flour and sauté for 1 minute.
2. Slowly add the milk while stirring continously so that lumps do not form. Bring to a boil.
3. Add the salt, pepper and cheese and mix well. Remove from the flame.

How to proceed
1. Grease a 150 mm. (6") diameter baking dish.
2. Place one sheet of lasagne on the baking dish.
3. Top with a layer of the eggplant, zucchini, garlic and parsley and then half of the tomato sauce.
4. Repeat with the second layer of the lasagne, eggplant, zucchini, garlic and parsley and the remaining tomato sauce.
5. Top with the third layer of the lasagne sheet. Pour the white sauce over so that the lasagne is covered completely.
6. Sprinkle with the grated cheese and bake in a pre-heated oven at 180°C (360°F) for 25 minutes.
   Serve hot.

RATATOUILLE RAVIOLI WITH TOMATO CREAM SAUCE

Picture on page 85

Ravioli is one of the best-known stuffed pasta dishes, famous beyond the shores of Italy. It is said that ravioli originally came from Liguria and was invented to use up left-over food.

This recipe of small square envelopes of pasta dough enclosing a mixed vegetable stuffing served with a tomato sauce, spiked with oregano and chilli is sure to tickle the Indian palate which craves for spices.

You can divide the making of ravioli into easy stages that can be completed well in advance. Make the filling and the sauce one day, then make the pasta dough and shape the ravioli the next day.

Remember to toss the ravioli in the sauce just before serving and then to eat it quickly!

 Preparation time : 30 minutes. Cooking time : 25 minutes. Serves 4.

For the ratatouille filling
¼ cup zucchini, finely chopped
¼ cup eggplant (baingan), finely chopped
¼ cup capsicum, finely chopped
¼ cup onions, finely chopped
1 teaspoon garlic, finely chopped
½ cup tomatoes, finely chopped
½ teaspoon dried oregano
1 tablespoon olive oil or oil
salt to taste

For the ravioli
1 recipe spinach (vegetable) pasta dough, page 138
1 teaspoon salt and 1 tablespoon oil for cooking the pasta

For the tomato cream sauce
1½ cups tomato pulp
1 tablespoon garlic, finely chopped
1 onion, finely chopped
2 tablespoons tomato purée
1 teaspoon sugar
½ teaspoon dried oregano
4 to 5 tablespoons cream
3 tablespoons olive oil or oil
salt to taste

For the garnish
2 tablespoons grated cheese
½ teaspoon chilli flakes

For the ratatouille filling
1. Heat the olive oil in a pan, add the zucchini, eggplant, capsicum, onions and garlic and sauté for 2 minutes.
2. Add the tomatoes and salt and cook on a slow flame till the moisture evaporates (approximately 5 to 7 minutes).
3. Sprinkle the oregano and mix well. Allow to cool completely.

For the ravioli
1. Divide the pasta dough into 2 portions and roll out each portion as thinly as possible without breaking the sheet.
2. Brush one sheet with cold water and place the ratatouille filling in little heaps (using a teaspoon) on it at regular intervals.
3. Cover with the second sheet of pasta and press around each mound of filling (as shown in the diagram below).
4. Cut with a small cookie cutter or knife into squares of 30 mm. x 30 mm. (1¼"x 1¼") and keep aside.
5. Boil plenty of water in a large saucepan with 1 teaspoon of salt and 1 tablespoon of oil added to it. Drop the ravioli in it piece by piece and cook a few pieces at a time for about 3 minutes.
6. Drain the ravioli and transfer it into a bowl of cold water to refresh it.
7. Drain again and keep aside.

For the tomato cream sauce

1. Heat the olive oil in a pan, add the garlic and onion and sauté till the onion turns translucent.
2. Add the tomato pulp and cook till the sauce thickens.
3. Add the tomato purée, sugar, salt and ½ cup of water and bring to a boil.
4. Add the oregano and cream and mix well. Keep aside.

How to proceed

1. Heat the tomato cream sauce and spoon it onto a plate.
2. Top with the ravioli and garnish with the cheese and chilli flakes.

HANDY TIPS
1. If the ravioli has turned cold, refresh it by immersing it in hot water for a few seconds.
2. Tomato pulp is made by blanching whole tomatoes in hot water and thereafter peeling, deseeding and chopping them.

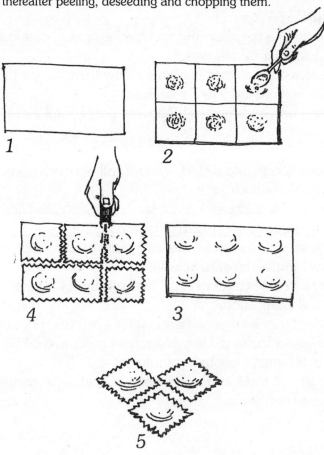

SPAGHETTI WITH EGGPLANT PARMAGIANNA

Picture on page 52

This famous pasta dish comes from Parma in Italy.
Spaghetti tossed in a chilli cream sauce topped with cheese filled eggplants and the
famous Italian tomato sauce. It makes a harmonious blend of flavours.
When selecting eggplants, look for those that are heavy for their size and have a
smooth, shiny and deep purple skin.
Toss the spaghetti in the chilli cream sauce just before serving, as it doesn't taste
as good when it is reheated. Warm the dish in an oven if the eggplant slices have
turned cold. Enjoy it hot and, of course, freshly prepared.

 Preparation time : 15 minutes. Cooking time : 30 minutes. Serves 4.

For the chilli cream spaghetti
3 cups cooked spaghetti, page 138
2 cloves garlic, sliced
1 tablespoon chilli flakes
½ cup milk
2 tablespoons cream
1 tomato, deseeded and chopped
1 teaspoon butter
1 teaspoon olive oil or oil
salt to taste

For the eggplant parmagianna
250 grams eggplant (baingan)
4 cheese slices
1 cup dried bread crumbs
½ teaspoon mixed dried herbs
½ teaspoon salt
¼ cup plain flour (maida)
oil for deep frying

Other ingredients
½ recipe tomato cream sauce, page 77

For the eggplant parmagianna
1. Slice the eggplant into 16 slices of 4 mm. thickness. Keep aside.
2. Combine the breadcrumbs, mixed herbs and salt in a dry plate and mix well.
3. Mix the flour with enough water in a bowl to make a paste of coating consistency.
4. Cut each slice of cheese to fit into the eggplant slice.
5. Place each portion of the cheese slice and 1 teaspoon of tomato cream sauce in between two eggplant slices.
6. Dip each eggplant cheese sandwich into the flour paste and then coat with the bread crumb mixture.
7. Press the bread crumbs firmly onto the eggplant slices.
8. Deep fry in hot oil till golden brown. Drain on absorbent paper and keep aside.

For the chilli cream spaghetti
1. Heat the butter and olive oil in a pan and sauté the garlic and chilli flakes in it for a few seconds.
2. Add the milk and cream and bring to a boil.
3. Add the spaghetti and salt and toss lightly.
4. Add the tomato and mix well. Keep aside.

How to proceed
1. Place the chilli cream spaghetti on a large serving plate and top with the eggplant parmagianna.
2. Heat the tomato cream sauce and pour on top.
   Serve hot.

GARLIC BASIL RAVIOLI WITH ALFREDO SAUCE

Ravioli, a pillow shaped pasta popular in several Italian regions is usually made with a stuffing of spinach and cheese.

Alfredo's was a popular restaurant in Rome where the chef's fresh pasta was served with a cheese and cream sauce. This sauce from Alfredo's served over pasta has become known as Alfredo sauce.

This recipe of ravioli uses refreshing green garlic and basil flavoured pasta dough filled with tomatoes, tossed with Alfredo sauce. You can also serve this ravioli tossed in butter and topped with parmesan cheese.

To prevent ravioli from losing its shape and filling, do not overcook it. Drain the tomatoes completely before stuffing them to prevent the ravioli from getting soggy.

 Preparation time : 30 minutes. Cooking time : 25 minutes. Serves 4.

For the ravioli
1 cup plain flour (maida)
2 tablespoons fresh green garlic, chopped
2 tablespoons fresh basil, chopped
4 tablespoons olive oil or oil
salt to taste
1 teaspoon salt and 1 tablespoon oil for cooking the pasta

For the filling
2 blanched tomatoes, peeled, deseeded and finely chopped
salt to taste

For the Alfredo sauce
1 tablespoon plain flour (maida)
2 tablespoons butter
2 cups milk
1 tablespoon white wine (optional)
¼ cup cheese, grated
salt to taste

For the ravioli

1. Sieve the flour and salt. Add the fresh green garlic, basil and olive oil.
2. Knead into a smooth but firm dough adding a little cold water if necessary.
3. Cover the dough with a wet muslin cloth and allow to rest for about 15 minutes.
4. Divide the dough into two portions and roll out each portion as thinly as possible without breaking the sheet.
5. Brush one sheet with cold water and place the chopped tomatoes in little heaps (using a teaspoon) on it at regular intervals.
6. Cover with the second sheet of pasta and press around each mound of filling as shown in the illustration on page 78.
7. Cut with a small cookie cutter or knife into squares of 36 mm. x 36 mm. (1½" x 1½") and keep aside.
8. Boil plenty of water in a large saucepan with 1 teaspoon of salt and 1 tablespoon of oil added to it. Drop the ravioli into it, a few pieces at a time and cook for 3 minutes.
9. Drain the ravioli and transfer into a bowl of cold water to refresh it.
10. Drain again and keep aside.

For the Alfredo sauce

1. Heat the butter in a saucepan, add the flour and sauté for 1 minute.
2. Gradually, pour the milk into it stirring continuously taking care to see that no lumps form. Bring to a boil.
3. Add the white wine, cheese and salt, mix well and keep aside.

How to proceed

Heat the Alfredo sauce and toss the ravioli in it.
Serve hot.

 Fresh green garlic is available in the winter. You can also substitute it with 1 tablespoon of grated garlic.

TORTELLINI WITH SUN-DRIED TOMATO PESTO SAUCE

Tortellini, the little rings of pasta filled with cheese, originated in the city of Bologna. Sun-dried tomatoes are extensively used all over the sunny Mediterranean regions of Italy. Sun-dried tomato pesto has the characteristic sharpness of tomatoes, along with the overpowering taste of garlic. You can prepare the tortellini a few hours in advance but be sure to mix in a tablespoon of oil to prevent them from sticking together. Seal it well in a bowl before storing. This recipe is a lovely combination of assertive flavours that harmonise together perfectly.

 Preparation time : 30 minutes. Cooking time : 30 minutes. Serves 4.

For the tortellini
1 recipe fresh pasta dough, page 137
1 teaspoon salt and 1 tablespoon oil for cooking the pasta

To be mixed into a cheese filling
1 cup cheese, grated
1 teaspoon mixed dried herbs

For the sauce
1 recipe sun-dried tomato pesto, page 141
1 teaspoon chilli powder
1 cup fresh cream
1 cup milk
salt to taste

For the tortellini
1. Divide the pasta dough into two equal portions and roll out each portion as thinly as you can without breaking the sheet.
2. Using a 50 mm. (2") diameter cookie cutter, cut into circles.
3. Place ¼ teaspoon of the cheese filling in little heaps in the centre of each circle.

4. Brush the sides of the circle with a little cold water and join them together by pressing the edges firmly (refer to the diagram below).
5. Brush the corners of the semi-circle with cold water and join them together by pressing the edges firmly (refer to the diagram below).
6. Cook the tortellini, a few pieces at a time, for 3 to 4 minutes in a large pan of boiling water to which 1 teaspoon of salt and 1 tablespoon of oil has been added.
7. Drain and transfer the tortellini into a bowl of cold water to refresh it. Drain again and keep aside.

For the sauce
1. Combine the sun-dried tomato pesto, chilli powder, fresh cream, milk and salt in a large saucepan and mix well. Allow to simmer for 5 to 6 minutes while stirring continuously.
2. Remove from the fire and keep aside.

How to proceed
Just before serving, re-heat the sauce and toss the tortellini in it.
Serve immediately.

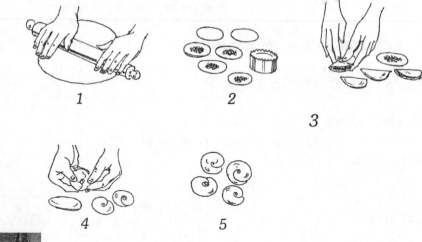

1. Peach Lettuce Salad, *page 46*
2. Ratatouille Ravioli with Tomato Cream Sauce, *page 76*

SPINACH & COTTAGE CHEESE CANNELONI

Spinach and cottage cheese stuffed in tubular pasta or cannelloni covered with oodles of cheese always finds its way in dinner menus! Well made cannelloni cannot be achieved without some effort, but the results are always superb. Basically there are four separate elements : the stuffing, the fresh pasta in which the stuffing is enclosed, the cheese that covers and protects the filled cannelloni as it heats and the sauce. The filling and the sauce can be prepared a day in advance, then assembled just before serving. Ready-made dry pasta sheets can be purchased to shorten the cooking process.

 Preparation time : 30 minutes. Cooking time : 30 minutes. Serves 4.

For the cannelloni
1 recipe fresh pasta dough, page 137
1 teaspoon salt and 1 tablespoon oil for cooking the pasta

For the spinach stuffing
3 cups spinach leaves, chopped
1 cup crumbled cottage cheese (paneer)
½ teaspoon chopped green chillies
a pinch nutmeg (jaiphal) powder
3 tablespoons cream
salt to taste

For the white sauce
3 tablespoons plain flour (maida)
3 tablespoons butter

1. Olive Cream Cheese Dip, *page 27*
2. Green Tagliatelle with Mushrooms & Broccoli, *page 70*

3 cups milk
salt and pepper to taste

Other ingredients
2 tablespoons grated cheese
butter or oil for greasing

For the spinach stuffing
1. Blanch the spinach in boiling water. Refresh in ice-cold water and drain out the water. Keep aside.
2. Chop finely and mix with the cottage cheese, green chillies, nutmeg powder, cream and salt. Keep aside.

For the cannelloni
1. Prepare the pasta dough as mentioned in the recipe.
2. Divide the pasta dough into 6 portions and roll out each portion as thinly as possible.
3. Cut each portion of the rolled out dough into a 100 mm. x 150 mm. (4" x 6") rectangle, to make 6 cannelloni sheets.
4. Boil plenty of water in a broad pan and add 1 teaspoon of salt and 1 tablespoon of oil.
5. Drop the prepared pasta one sheet at a time into the boiling water and cook for 2 minutes.
6. Drain and transfer into a bowl of cold water. Drain again and keep aside.

For the white sauce
1. Heat the butter, add the flour and sauté for 1 minute.
2. Slowly pour in the milk, whisking it continuously so that no lumps form. Bring to a boil.
3. Add salt and pepper and mix well. Remove from the fire.

How to proceed
1. Fill each cannelloni sheet with 1 tablespoon of the spinach stuffing and roll up.
2. Arrange on a greased baking dish, pour the white sauce over the prepared cannelloni and sprinkle grated cheese on top.
3. Bake in a pre-heated oven at 200°C (400°F) for 15 minutes.
   Serve hot.

QUICK
READY-MADE PASTA

There are so many varieties of pasta that it's easy
to be confused about which sauce will go with which
pasta. In this section, I have listed out my favourite
combinations. But the general rule is that thin pasta
like spaghetti go well with smoother creamier sauces
while pasta like penne and macaroni go well with
chunky and more robust sauces as these pastas can
hold the sauce well. The ridges on the outer surface
of thicker pasta are there so that the sauce can hold
on to the pasta. All of these are relatively easy to make.
Just collect all your ingredients together before you
start the actual cooking.

BASIL & TOMATO PASTA

Pasta is always served with a sauce in Southern Italy and the sauce invariably includes tomatoes, onions and garlic amongst its ingredients.

Basil and tomato sauce is arguably one of the best known pasta sauces of Italy. Bow tie pasta or farfalle is accompanied with this famous basil and red tomato sauce.

You can prepare larger quantities of this sauce and freeze it. Parboiled vegetables can also be added to this recipe.

 Preparation time : 15 minutes. Cooking time : 15 minutes. Serves 4.

3 cups cooked bow pasta (farfalle), page 138

For the basil and tomato sauce
1½ cups tomato pulp
1 tablespoon garlic, chopped
1 onion, finely chopped
1 teaspoon chilli powder
2 tablespoons tomato purée
1 teaspoon sugar
4 to 5 tablespoons fresh cream
12 to 15 basil leaves, chopped
2 tablespoons olive oil or butter
salt to taste

For the garnish
4 tablespoons grated parmesan cheese or processed cheese
a few basil leaves

For the basil and tomato sauce
1. Heat the olive oil in a pan, add the garlic
   and onion and sauté till the onion turns translucent.
2. Add the tomato pulp and cook till the sauce thickens
   (approx. 5 to 7 minutes).

3. Add the chilli powder, tomato purée, sugar, salt and ½ cup of water and bring to a boil.
4. Add the cream and basil leaves. Mix well and keep aside.

How to proceed
1. Just before serving, re-heat the basil and tomato sauce and toss the bow pasta in it.
2. Serve hot, garnished with the cheese and basil leaves.

 HANDY TIP   Tomato pulp is made by blanching whole tomatoes in hot water and thereafter peeling, deseeding and chopping them.

S P A G H E T T I   V E R D I

Spaghetti tossed in a spinach and cheese sauce with colourful vegetables makes a delightful recipe.
The beautiful green colour and good coating quality of the sauce makes it useful when serving along with pasta for a lunch or dinner.
The cheese spread blends beautifully to give a thick and creamy sauce.
To retain the fresh green colour of spinach, blanch the spinach and refresh quickly in ice-cold water. You may add a pinch of soda bi-carb to the water in which the spinach is to be boiled. This also helps to retain the green colour of spinach.

 Preparation time : 10 minutes. Cooking time : 15 minutes. Serves 4.

3 cups cooked spaghetti, page 138

For the sauce
4 cups spinach leaves, finely chopped
1 cup spring onions with greens, finely chopped
3 cloves garlic, finely chopped
½ cup red pepper, sliced
½ cup cheese spread
1½ cups milk
3 tablespoons butter
salt and pepper to taste

For the sauce

1. Blanch the spinach in boiling water for one minute. Drain and refresh in ice-cold water. Drain again and purée in a blender. Keep aside.
2. Heat the butter in a pan, add the spring onions and garlic and sauté for 2 to 3 minutes.
3. Add the red pepper and sauté for another 2 to 3 minutes.
4. Add the spinach purée, cheese spread, milk, salt and pepper and mix well. Bring it to a boil while stirring continuously. Remove and keep aside.

How to proceed

Just before serving, re-heat the sauce, adding a little milk or water if required and toss the spaghetti in the sauce.
Serve hot.

PASTA GENOVESE

Genovese is one of the great sauces of Italy. The city of Genoa in Italy takes the credit of creating this sauce which uses the famous "pesto" (also originated in Genoa). This sauce is traditionally served with pasta.
The addition of mushrooms enhances the taste of this already flavourful sauce.
Pesto can be easily made at home — by pounding basil, garlic, walnuts and olive oil or you can buy ready-made pesto, available at speciality gourmet stores.

 Preparation time : 15 minutes. Cooking time : 20 minutes. Serves 4.

3 cups cooked fettuccine, page 138

For the sauce

1 recipe pesto, page 140
1 onion, sliced
1½ cups mushrooms, sliced
1 cup milk
4 tablespoons cream
½ cup grated cheese
3 tablespoons butter
salt and pepper to taste

1. Heat the butter in a pan and sauté the onion slices till they are translucent.
2. Add the mushrooms and salt and sauté for 3 to 4 minutes.
3. Add the pesto, milk and cream and mix well. Bring to a boil while stirring continuously.
4. Toss in the pasta, pepper and cheese and serve immediately.

 HANDY TIP You can add your favourite vegetables like carrots, broccoli, french beans etc. to this dish. Just parboil them before you add them.

GARDEN FRESH FUSILLI

Simple classic pasta made with fusilli and cottage cheese tossed along with garden fresh parsley and basil enhances the essence of each and every ingredient used. You can replace the fusilli with penne, conchiglie or any other short pasta. This recipe is a good choice for an easy lunch menu. Fresh herbs have a magical and concentrated flavour and bring a dazzling green effect on the pasta.

Preparation time : 5 minutes. Cooking time : 10 minutes. Serves 4.

3 cups cooked fusilli, page 138
2 cloves garlic, finely chopped
2 green chillies, finely chopped
1½ cups cottage cheese (paneer), cut into cubes
½ cup milk
1 cup fresh parsley, finely chopped
½ cup fresh basil leaves, finely chopped
2 tablespoons cream
1 tablespoon butter
1 tablespoon olive oil or oil
salt to taste

1. Heat the butter and olive oil in a pan and add the garlic and green chillies to it.
2. Add the paneer cubes and stir for some time.
3. Add all the remaining ingredients and mix gently.
4. Bring to a boil and serve hot.

HANDY TIP 👉 Make this pasta just before you are ready to serve it. Keep the ingredients ready in advance.

SPAGHETTI PUTTANESCA

The ladies of the night in Naples are credited with inventing this dish. They liked it because it is fast, easy to cook and uses very few ingredients. I think you will like it too! Spaghetti tossed with garlic, tomatoes and olives make this a quick and classic combination.

 Preparation time : 10 minutes. Cooking time : 10 minutes. Serves 4.

3 cups cooked spaghetti, page 138

For the sauce
4 cloves garlic, chopped
¼ cup capsicum, cut into small pieces
2 tablespoons celery, chopped
2 cups tomatoes, chopped
1 teaspoon mixed dried herbs
1 teaspoon chilli flakes
10 to 12 black olives, sliced
2 tablespoons red wine (optional)
4 tablespoons olive oil or oil
salt and pepper to taste

For the garnish
4 tablespoons grated parmesan cheese or processed cheese

1. Heat the olive oil in a pan and sauté the garlic and capsicum in it for about 1 minute.
2. Add the celery, tomatoes and salt and mix well.
3. Add the mixed herbs, chilli flakes, olives and pepper and sauté for 4 to 5 minutes.
4. Toss in the spaghetti and red wine and mix well.
   Serve immediately, garnished with the parmesan cheese.

FUSILLI WITH RED PEPPER SAUCE

Romans often make this delicate preparation of pasta tossed with a lightly flavoured red pepper sauce spiked with herbs and jalapenos.

As with many recipes where there are a few ingredients, it is the quality of the ingredients which makes the difference between a mediocre dish and an exceptional one. Choose firm and deep red coloured peppers, as they are sweeter and more concentrated in flavour. The result will be a more flavourful and brighter coloured sauce.

You can replace the fusilli with any other short pasta like penne, conchiglie. You can even try the red pepper sauce with a filled pasta like tortellini or ravioli. The choice is yours.

Preparation time : 5 minutes.   Cooking time : 15 minutes.   Serves 4.

3 cups cooked fusilli, page 138

For the red pepper sauce
3 large red peppers
2 onions, sliced
4 cloves garlic, chopped
¼ cup cream
1 teaspoon mixed dried herbs
4 pickled jalapenos, chopped
2 tablespoons olive oil or oil
salt and pepper to taste

For the garnish
½ cup cheese, grated

For the red pepper sauce
1. Cut and deseed the red peppers.
2. Blanch in hot water and drain.

3. Heat the olive oil in a pan and sauté the onions and garlic till the onions are translucent.
4. Combine the blanched peppers, onions and garlic in a blender and purée to a smooth sauce.
5. Transfer into a saucepan and add the cream, mixed herbs, jalapenos, salt and pepper and bring to a boil.
6. Remove from the fire and keep aside.

How to proceed

1. Just before serving, re-heat the red pepper sauce, toss the fusilli in it and mix well.
2. Serve immediately, garnished with the grated cheese.

FUSILLI WITH BABY CORN & WALNUTS

Fusilli is a short twisted pasta from Southern Italy usually served with a spicy tomato sauce. Originating from Naples, it is also known as "Eliche" or "propellers" for its quality of trapping particles of the sauce and "propelling" them to the tongue. This recipe uses fusilli tossed along with baby corn, walnuts with a sprinkling of fresh basil and parsley.
An enticing blend of flavours! Toss this pasta as close to serving time as possible as it tastes best then.

 Preparation time : 10 minutes. Cooking time : 10 minutes. Serves 4.

3 cups cooked fusilli, page 138
1 onion finely, finely chopped
3 cloves garlic, finely chopped
¼ cup walnuts, finely chopped
1 cup baby corn, sliced
2 tablespoons parsley, finely chopped

2 tablespoons fresh basil, finely chopped
a pinch nutmeg (jaiphal)
4 tablespoons olive oil or butter
salt and freshly ground pepper to taste

For serving
3 tablespoons grated parmesan cheese or processed cheese

1. Heat the olive oil in a pan, add the onion and garlic and sauté till the onion turns translucent.
2. Add the walnuts and baby corn and sauté for 3 to 4 minutes.
3. Add the fusilli, parsley, basil, nutmeg, salt and pepper and toss well. Serve hot garnished with the cheese.

PENNE WITH SPRING ONIONS, CORN & RED PEPPER

Picture on page 25

The word "penne" means "feather" indicating the transversely cut shape of the pasta which resembles the wing of a bird. Penne tossed along with spring onions, corn and pepper is simply superb. You will find this a wonderful dish for family meals. I bet you will find yourself using this easy recipe time and time again.

 Preparation time : 5 minutes. Cooking time : 10 minutes. Serves 4.

3 cups cooked penne, page 138
4 cups spring onions (including greens), finely chopped
2 cloves garlic, sliced
¼ cup sweet corn kernels
4 to 5 sun-dried tomatoes, page 142, soaked and sliced
1 red pepper, cut into thin slices
2 tablespoons celery, chopped
4 tablespoons butter
salt and freshly ground pepper to taste

For serving

3 tablespoons grated parmesan cheese or processed cheese
1 teaspoon chilli flakes

1. Heat the butter in a pan, add the spring onions, garlic and corn and sauté for 4 to 5 minutes until the corn is cooked.
2. Add the penne, sun-dried tomatoes, red pepper, celery, salt and pepper and toss well.
   Serve hot, topped with the cheese and chilli flakes.

CHEESY MACARONI WITH BROCCOLI

No Neapolitan meal is ever complete without a dish of macaroni. Macaroni was invented in this region and the word today has almost become generic for dried pasta. Although known elsewhere in Italy as "maccheroni", macaroni is the spelling used in Naples and throughout Europe.

Macaroni tossed in a cream and cheese sauce with fresh broccoli is a delightful recipe. Toss and serve this pasta immediately as it does not taste very well when it is re-heated.

 Preparation time : 10 minutes. Cooking time : 10 minutes. Serves 4.

3 cups cooked macaroni, page 138
2 cloves garlic, chopped
2 cups broccoli, cut into florets
1 tablespoon fresh basil, chopped
⅓ cup milk
¼ cup cream
½ cup grated cheese
2 tablespoons butter
salt and freshly ground pepper to taste

1. Melt the butter in a saucepan, add the garlic and broccoli and sauté for 2 minutes.
2. Add the basil, milk, cream, salt and pepper and bring to a boil.
3. Add the macaroni and cheese and toss lightly.
   Serve hot.

Rice and Gnocchi

Rice is not eaten as an accompaniment in Italy, but as a first course. Risotto is made with special kind of short grained rice called "arborio" which is extremely absorbent. This variety of rice gives the dish its creamy consistency and yet all the grains of rice are separate. The perfect end result is also achieved by cooking on a slow flame and gradually adding the liquid or stock as required. Frequent stirring is essential to avoid the rice grains sticking. Gnocchi are little dumplings that are either poached or steamed. The shapes of gnocchi also vary from spheres to elongated cylinders. Gnocchi are served with a sauce or simply tossed in garlic, butter and cheese. Smaller gnocchi are also sometimes added to soups or casseroles. Try these combinations.
I'm sure you'll enjoy them.

ROASTED VEGETABLES WITH BROWN RICE

Rice is popularly eaten in all regions of Northern Italy whereas pasta is popular in the South.

This recipe is a great supper dish of caramelised onion rice topped with garlic roasted vegetables and a creamy cheese sauce.

Caramelising onions gives the rice a light brown colour and sautéing the rice in oil helps to keep the rice grains separate when they are cooked. Long grained rice when cooked is aromatic and flavourful and is best suited for this recipe.

Oven roasted vegetables have a unique flavour that sautéed vegetables cannot match with a predominant garlic taste.

 Preparation time : 15 minutes. Cooking time : 50 minutes. Serves 4.

For the brown rice
1 cup long grained rice
1 onion, sliced
2 cloves garlic, chopped
2 tablespoons olive oil or oil
salt to taste

For the roasted vegetables
3 cups mixed vegetables (broccoli, carrots, red and green capsicum, baby corn), cut into 25 mm. (1") pieces
4 cloves garlic, chopped
1 tablespoon olive oil or oil
salt to taste

For the cheese sauce
2 tablespoons plain flour (maida)
2 tablespoons butter
2 cups milk
1 teaspoon chilli flakes
½ cup grated cheese
½ teaspoon dried mixed herbs
salt and pepper to taste

For the brown rice
1. Clean, wash and soak the rice for 10 minutes. Drain and keep aside.
2. Heat the olive oil in a pan, add the onion and sauté till the onion is browned. Add the garlic and sauté for another 2 minutes.
3. Add the rice and salt and sauté for a further 3 to 4 minutes.
4. Add 2 cups of hot water, cover the pan with a lid and simmer over a slow flame till the rice is cooked. Keep aside.

For the roasted vegetables
1. Combine the vegetables, garlic, olive oil and salt in a baking tray. Toss well.
2. Bake in pre-heated oven at 200°C (400°F) for 15 to 20 minutes, stirring once in between till they are slightly brown in colour. Keep aside.

For the cheese sauce
1. Melt the butter in a pan, add the flour and sauté for 1 minute.
2. Gradually add the milk and 1 cup of water, stirring continuously so that no lumps form. Bring to a boil.
3. Remove from the fire, add the chilli flakes, cheese, mixed herbs, salt and pepper and stir well. Keep aside.

How to proceed
1. Arrange a layer of the brown rice in a 200 mm. (8") diameter baking dish.
2. Cover with a layer of the roasted vegetables and top with the cheese sauce.
3. Just before serving, bake in a pre-heated oven at 220°C (430°F) for 10 to 15 minutes.
Serve hot.

MILANESE SUN-DRIED TOMATO RISOTTO

The mention of Milan produces immediate thoughts of the wonderful risotto named after the city.

Risottos are best made using a special kind of Italian rice called "arborio" which is cooked with stock, garlic and a wide variety of other ingredients.

The trick to prepare a perfect risotto is slow cooking of rice and judicious stirring. I have replaced arborio rice with a long grained rice although its texture will not be the same. There is however no substitute to sun-dried tomatoes. Their chewy, salty taste enhances this risotto beyond words. Although it may sound very complicated, sun-dried tomatoes are relatively easy to prepare at home by following the recipe on page 142. The risotto must be prepared as close to serving time as possible as it is best when freshly prepared.

 Preparation time : 15 minutes. Cooking time : 15 minutes. Serves 3 to 4.

1 cup long grained rice
2 cloves garlic, finely chopped
1 medium onion, finely chopped
½ cup white wine (optional)
1 cup seasoning cube (vegetarian)
1 cup broccoli, cut into small florets
¼ cup sun-dried tomatoes, page 142, soaked and thinly sliced
1 teaspoon dried oregano
1 teaspoon chilli flakes
¼ cup grated cheese
2 tablespoons cream
2 tablespoons butter
salt to taste

1. Clean, wash and soak the rice for about 10 minutes. Drain and keep aside.
2. Heat the butter in a pan, add the garlic and onion and sauté for 2 minutes.
3. Add the rice and sauté for a further 1 minute.
4. Add the white wine, seasoning cube and salt and bring to a boil.
5. Add 4 cups of hot water, cover and cook on a slow flame for about 5 to 7 minutes.
6. Add the broccoli, sun-dried tomatoes, oregano and chilli flakes and mix well.
7. Simmer till all the moisture has evaporated and the rice has cooked.
8. Add the grated cheese and cream and mix well.
   Serve immediately.

RISOTTO FIORENTINA

Picture on page 51

In Italy, the term "alla fiorentina" is used for dishes that are typically connected to the city of Florence. Florentine is a style of cooking pasta, rice and vegetables in which spinach is essentially used.

Risotto fiorentina is a classic preparation of cheesy creamy Italian rice cooked in stock and topped with cooked spinach, tomato purée and fresh Italian herbs— basil and parsley.

Italian rice used for risotto is a round, short grained variety with a nutty flavour. Arborio rice is the very best kind to use. Risotto is best when freshly prepared and quickly eaten!

 Preparation time : 10 minutes. Cooking time : 20 minutes. Serves 4.

1 cup long grained rice
¼ cup finely chopped carrots
¼ cup green peas
1 teaspoon chopped garlic
1 cup spinach, blanched, drained and finely chopped
2 tablespoons fresh basil, chopped
2 tablespoons finely chopped celery
1 tablespoon finely chopped parsley
½ cup grated cheese
⅓ cup tomato purée
2 tablespoons fresh cream
2 to 3 tablespoons red wine (optional)
3 tablespoons olive oil or oil
salt to taste

1. Clean, wash and soak the rice for about 10 minutes. Drain and keep aside.
2. Heat the olive oil in a pan, add the carrots, green peas and garlic and sauté for 2 minutes.
3. Add the rice and sauté for 2 minutes.
4. Pour 3½ cups of hot water and salt and bring to a boil. Cover and simmer till the rice is almost cooked, adding a little water if required.
5. When the rice is cooked, add the spinach, basil, celery, parsley, cheese, tomato pureé, cream and red wine and mix well.

Serve immediately.

 HANDY TIP Toss in the greens (i.e. spinach, basil and parsley) just before you are ready to serve the risotto or they will discolour.

SPINACH GNOCCHI WITH ALMOND BUTTER SAUCE

Gnocchi are almost easier to make than to pronounce "n-yoki". The word means "lumps" because of the irregular, somewhat craggy shapes these dumplings have. Gnocchi are boiled in the same fashion as pasta is and are served generally with a cream based sauce.

Spinach and cottage cheese gnocchi served in a toasted almond and butter sauce makes an outstanding first course. Alternatively, try gnocchi as a rich and creamy side dish. Make sure you drain out all the water from the spinach before you make the gnocchi.

Test one gnocchi by boiling it in water. If it crumbles, add some more flour to the mixture.

Always make the gnocchi the day you are going to serve them because they will discolour if left overnight. Also prepare the sauce just before you are ready to eat!

 Preparation time : 10 minutes. Cooking time : 20 minutes. Serves 4.

For the spinach gnocchi
4 cups chopped spinach
1 cup grated paneer (cottage cheese)
¼ teaspoon nutmeg (jaiphal) powder
4 tablespoons plain flour (maida)
⅛ teaspoon baking powder
salt to taste
1 teaspoon salt and 1 tablespoon oil for cooking the gnocchi

For the almond butter sauce
6 tablespoons butter

For the spinach gnocchi

1. Blanch the spinach in boiling water for 1 minute. Drain and refresh in ice-cold water. Drain again and squeeze out all the water.
2. Chop the spinach finely.
3. Combine all the ingredients in a bowl and mix well to form a soft dough.
4. Divide the gnocchi into approximately 30 equal sized balls.
5. Press each one gently to flatten using a fork.
6. Boil plenty of water in a broad pan and add 1 teaspoon of salt and 1 tablespoon of oil to it.
7. When the water is boiling, add the gnocchi a few pieces at a time and allow them to cook for 3 to 4 minutes.
8. Carefully remove the gnocchi from the boiling water, using a slotted spoon. Keep aside.

For the almond butter sauce

1. Heat the butter in a pan and sauté the almonds till they are lightly toasted.
2. Season with pepper and keep aside.

How to proceed

Just before serving, toss the gnocchi in the almond butter sauce and mix well. Serve immediately.

 HANDY TIPS 1.While cooking the gnocchi, boil one first to see that it does not crumble in the water. If it does, add some more flour.
2. If you want the gnocchi to be a little spicy, add 1 to 2 finely chopped green chillies.

POTATO GNOCCHI WITH MUSHROOM BASIL SAUCE

Once again it is the Italians who are so clever at inventing such simple things out of what seem to be fairly ordinary ingredients but then become something quite outstanding. Thus it is with the gnocchi   little dumplings made out of potato, flour and seasoning, just like they are made in Piedmont, Italy.

They seem very ordinary, but are quite exquisite when made in the old-fashioned way. Gnocchi have a texture and flavour of their own and complement the sauces they are tossed in.

This dish is very simple, served with a fresh garlic and mushroom sauce aromatised with basil.

Gnocchi are cooked just the way pasta is viz. boiled in plenty of water. When the gnocchi begin to float to the surface of the water, they are cooked. Use old potatoes that have a lower water content and will cook better.

Gnocchi are traditionally served as appetizers but when served with a salad or bread, they can make a substantial meal.

 Preparation time : 20 minutes. Cooking time : 30 minutes. Serves 4.

For the potato gnocchi
2 cups boiled potatoes, grated
6 tablespoons plain flour (maida)
salt and pepper to taste
1 teaspoon salt and 1 tablespoon oil for cooking the gnocchi

For the mushroom basil sauce
2 cups fresh mushrooms, finely chopped
1 large onion, finely chopped
4 large cloves garlic, finely chopped
¼ cup cream

2 tablespoons fresh basil, chopped
2 tablespoons butter
salt and freshly ground pepper to taste

For the potato gnocchi

1. Combine all the ingredients in a bowl and knead very well.
2. Divide the mixture into 30 to 40 equal portions.
3. Shape each portion into a cylindrical roll 25 mm. (1") in length. Lightly flatten each gnocchi using a fork (as shown in the diagram below). Keep aside.
4. Boil plenty of water in a large pan and add 1 teaspoon of salt and 1 tablespoon of oil to it. Drop a few pieces at a time of the prepared gnocchi in it and at allow to cook for 2 minutes.
5. Carefully remove the gnocchi from the boiling water, using a slotted spoon. Keep aside.

For the mushroom basil sauce

1. Heat the butter in a pan, add the onion and sauté till the onion turns translucent. Add the garlic and sauté for 1 minute.
2. Add the mushrooms and sauté for 3 to 4 minutes.
3. Add the cream, basil, salt, pepper and ¼ cup of water and mix well. Bring the sauce to a boil. Keep aside.

How to proceed

Just before serving, re-heat the mushroom basil sauce and toss the prepared potato gnocchi in it.
Serve hot.

HANDY TIP Test one gnocchi by boiling it in water. If the gnocchi breaks, you may need to add 1 to 2 tablespoons of flour in the gnocchi dough.

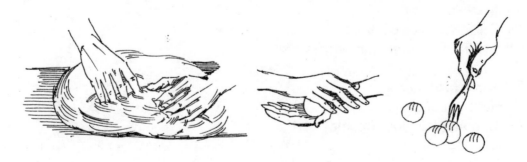

PUMPKIN GNOCCHI FLORENTINE

Picture on page 111

Pumpkin dumplings tossed in a crunchy walnut, spinach and cottage cheese sauce. Ground nutmeg adds a delightful new twist to this traditional favourite. Semolina is used for binding the gnocchi along with plain flour as it imparts a delicious texture to the gnocchi. Choose firm, rich, orange coloured pumpkin for good texture and flavour. Squeeze out all the water from the pumpkin after it has been boiled to reduce the amount of flour required to bind the gnocchi. You can prepare the gnocchi in advance and toss it in the sauce just when you are ready to serve it.

 Preparation time : 20 minutes. Cooking time : 20 minutes. Serves 4.

For the pumpkin gnocchi
2½ cups red pumpkin (kaddu), cubed
⅓ cup fine semolina (rava)
3 tablespoons plain flour (maida)
a pinch of nutmeg (jaiphal) powder
salt and freshly ground pepper to taste
1 teaspoon salt and 1 tablespoon oil for cooking the gnocchi

For the spinach mixture
2 cups spinach, blanched and finely chopped
1 cup crumbled paneer (cottage cheese)
2 tablespoons chopped walnuts
2 large onions, chopped
5 cloves garlic, finely chopped
¼ teaspoon nutmeg (jaiphal) powder
¼ cup cream
2 tablespoons olive oil or oil
salt and freshly ground pepper to taste

For the white sauce
1 tablespoon butter
2 teaspoons plain flour (maida)

½ cup milk
½ cup water
salt and freshly ground pepper to taste

For serving
½ cup grated cheese

For the pumpkin gnocchi
1. Pressure cook the pumpkin with ½ cup of water till it is tender. Drain and squeeze out all the water.
2. Mash the pumpkin using a fork. Add the semolina, flour, nutmeg, salt and pepper and mix well.
3. Divide the pumpkin mixture into approx. 30 equal sized balls.
4. Press each one gently to flatten it using a fork (as shown in the picture on page 111).
5. Boil plenty of water in a broad pan and add 1 teaspoon of salt and 1 tablespoon of oil to it.
6. When the water is boiling, add the gnocchi a few pieces at a time and allow them to cook for 3 to 4 minutes.
7. Carefully remove the gnocchi out of the boiling water, using a slotted spoon. Keep aside.

For the spinach mixture
1. Heat the olive oil in a pan, add the onions and sauté till they turn translucent. Add the garlic and sauté for another minute.
2. Add the spinach, paneer, walnuts, nutmeg, cream, salt and pepper and mix well. Stir for a few minutes till all the liquid evaporates.

For the white sauce
1. Heat the butter in a pan, add the flour and cook for 1 minute.
2. Gradually add the milk and water, stirring continuously so that lumps do not form and bring to a boil.
3. Add the salt and pepper and mix well. Keep aside.

How to proceed
1. In a large serving plate, spread the spinach mixture evenly.
2. Top with the pumpkin gnocchi and pour the white sauce over.

Sprinkle the cheese on top and serve immediately.

HANDY TIP ☞ Cook one gnocchi first. If it crumbles in the water, add some more flour to the gnocchi dough and mix well.

PIEDMONTESE GNOCCHI WITH TOMATO & RED WINE SAUCE

Piedmont, is a region in Italy bordering both France and Switzerland. Piedmontese food is a substantial, peasant type fare. Garlic features predominantly in their recipes.

Gnocchi are often offered as a first course when soup in not served.

In this recipe of Piedmontese Gnocchi, little potato vegetable dumplings are served tossed in a robust tomato and red wine sauce predominantly flavoured with garlic and oregano.

The rules of cooking and serving pasta and gnocchi are essentially the same i.e. boil in plenty of water. Serve the gnocchi freshly tossed in the tomato and red wine sauce.

For an exciting variation, try serving the gnocchi with a pesto sauce, page 92

 Preparation time : 15 minutes. Cooking time : 30 minutes. Serves 4.

1. Three Bean Salad, *page 44*
2. Pumpkin Gnocchi Florentine, *page 108*

For the vegetable potato gnocchi

½ cup boiled potatoes, grated
½ cup grated carrots
2 tablespoons finely chopped celery
6 tablespoons plain flour (maida)
salt and pepper to taste
1 teaspoon salt and 1 tablespoon oil for cooking the gnocchi

For the tomato and red wine sauce

1½ cups tomato pulp
1 tablespoon garlic, finely chopped
1 onion, finely chopped
2 tablespoons tomato purée
1 teaspoon sugar
½ teaspoon dried oregano
4 to 5 tablespoons cream
4 tablespoons red wine
3 tablespoons olive oil or butter
salt to taste

For the garnish

4 tablespoons grated cheese

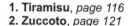
1. Tiramisu, *page 116*
2. Zuccoto, *page 121*

For the vegetable potato gnocchi

1. Combine all the ingredients in a bowl and knead very well.
2. Divide the mixture into 40 equal portions.
3. Shape each portion into a cylindrical roll 25 mm. (1") in length. Lightly flatten each gnocchi using a fork (as shown in the diagram on page 107). Keep aside.
4. Boil plenty of water on a large pan to which 1 teaspoon of salt and 1 tablespoon of oil has been added. Drop the prepared gnocchi in the boiling water a few pieces at a time and allow to cook for 2 minutes.
5. Carefully remove the gnocchi from the water using a slotted spoon. Keep aside.

For the tomato and red wine sauce

1. Heat the olive oil in a pan, add the garlic and onion and sauté till the onion turns translucent.
2. Add the tomato pulp and cook till the sauce thickens.
3. Add the tomato purée, sugar, salt and ½ cup of water and bring to a boil.
4. Add the oregano and cream and mix well.
5. Finish with the red wine and keep aside.

How to proceed

1. Just before serving, re-heat the sauce and toss the vegetable potato gnocchi in it.
2. Serve hot, garnished with the cheese.

 HANDY TIPS 1. Tomato pulp is made by blanching whole tomatoes in hot water and thereafter peeling, deseeding and chopping them.
2. For the gnocchi, use old potatoes or use a variety that has more starch and has less water content for best results.

DESSERTS

"Dolci" as the Italians would call dessert is not a part of every Italian meal. Although the Italians have a sweet tooth, dinners are mostly finished with fresh fruits and cheese. Cake and pastries are eaten at other times of the day. Possibly the only exception to these are "gelato" i.e. ice-creams, water ices and granitas which Italy is so renowned for. Italian pastry is rich but light, a skill that is difficult to achieve without some measure of skill and rich practice. Whether is the mascarpone-laden Tiramisu or the creamy Casatta. I'm sure you'll enjoy making these divine creations for your loved ones.

Bon appetit!

TIRAMISU

Picture on page 112

Italian cooking is never complete without the mention of this famed dessert that is as popular beyond the shores of Italy as it is within Italy.

Literally translated Tiramisu means "lift me up". Tira Mi Su was named for its restorative properties - cream, cheese and wine that were thought to be excellent for those in poor health. The addition of expresso should give a lift to those in the best of health!

Mascarpone traditionally used for this dessert is a rich, soft cheese. It is smooth and mild in texture and has originated in Northern Italy. Cream cheese has been substituted in place of mascarpone and gives equally good results.

Marsala, an amber coloured wine from Sicily, is a part of the traditional recipe. The sweeter variety is used for this dessert. Port wine has been found to be a good substitute if Marsala is not available.

You can arrange the Tiramisu in individual glasses instead of a serving dish. But this is a must try recipe to lift up spirits!

 Preparation time : 20 minutes. Cooking time : 20 minutes. Serves 4 to 6.
Setting time : 4 to 6 hours.

1 recipe sponge cake, page 121
½ recipe cream cheese, page 144
5 tablespoons sugar
¼ cup marsala or port wine
1 cup fresh cream
3 tablespoons icing sugar

To mixed into a coffee soaking syrup
1 teaspoon instant coffee powder
1 tablespoon sugar
4 tablespoons warm water

For the garnish
1 teaspoon cocoa powder

1. Cut a thin round of the sponge cake. Keep aside.
2. Cut the remaining sponge cake into 12 mm. x 50 mm. (½" x 2") long fingers.
3. Arrange the cake fingers on a baking tray and toast in a pre-heated oven at 160°C (320°F) for 20 minutes. Allow to cool.
4. In a pan, heat the marsala wine with the sugar over gentle heat until the sugar has dissolved. Allow it to cool.
5. Whip the cream with the icing sugar until soft peaks form. Keep refrigerated.
6. Whisk the cream cheese and wine mixture together. Gently fold in the whipped cream. Keep aside.
7. Arrange the cake round on the base of a 200 mm. (8") diameter serving dish. Soak generously with the coffee soaking syrup.
8. Top with half of the cream cheese mixture. Freeze for 30 minutes until it has set.
9. Dip each piece of toasted cake finger in the coffee soaking syrup for 10 seconds.
10. Arrange the soaked cake fingers over the first layer of cream cheese. Top with the remaining cream cheese mixture. Freeze for 4 to 6 hours until set.
11. Sprinkle the cocoa powder on top. Cut into squares and serve immediately.

WALNUT TART

The Italian fondness for pastries and tarts leads them to innovative, exciting and mouth-watering recipes.

This innovative recipe is of a crisp pastry enclosing a soft and chewy filling of cinnamon flavoured cake crumbs and walnuts which are bound with condensed milk.

You can prepare larger quantities of the tart pastry dough and freeze it.

Thaw the dough and prepare tarts quickly at any time.

If you like, you can use any other liqueur instead of brandy and use roasted almonds instead of walnuts.

Serve this tart hot with a scoop of ice-cream, a sweet ending to an elaborate meal.

 Preparation time : 15 minutes. Cooking time : 40 minutes. Serves 4.

For the tart dough
1½ cups plain flour (maida)
½ cup butter, frozen and cut into small pieces
1 tablespoon powdered sugar
a pinch of salt

For the filling
½ cup condensed milk
2 tablespoons jam
2 tablespoons milk
2 tablespoons brandy
2 cups chocolate cake crumbs, see below
½ cup walnuts, chopped
¼ teaspoon cinnamon powder

Other ingredients
milk for glazing

For the tart dough
1. Sieve the flour and salt together.
2. Rub the butter into the flour using your fingertips till the mixture resembles bread crumbs. Add the sugar and mix well.

3. Gradually, add enough ice-cold water (about 2 to 3 tablespoons) to make a dough. Refrigerate for 10 to 15 minutes.
4. Roll out ⅔ of the dough into a circle and line a 150 mm. (6") diameter tart mould.
5. Prick with a fork at regular intervals.
6. Roll out the (⅓) remaining dough into a circle of 200 mm. (8") diameter and keep aside.

For the filling
1. Melt the condensed milk, jam and milk in a non-stick pan over gentle heat.
2. Add the brandy, cake crumbs, walnuts and cinnamon powder and mix well. Keep aside.

How to proceed
1. Spoon the filling mixture into prepared tart mould.
2. Cover with the remaining rolled out (⅓) tart dough and seal the edges completely. Prick the top of the tart with a fork at regular intervals to allow the steam to escape.
3. Brush the tart with milk. Bake in a pre-heated oven at 180°C (360°F) for 25 to 30 minutes or until golden brown.
   Serve hot, with whipped cream or vanilla ice-cream.

 For the chocolate cake crumbs, use a day old chocolate sponge cake (follow the recipe on page 128)

MELON & STRAWBERRY GELATO

Italians have been in love with ices and ice-creams for hundreds of years. In Florence, during the Renaissance, special ice-houses were built so that cooks would always have the access to the ice needed to make their delicious desserts. Fruity and fresh flavours of this muskmelon and strawberry sorbet will cleanse your palate after a cheesy Italian meal, leaving you hungry for more!

 Preparation time : 10 minutes. No cooking. Serves 4. Setting time : 2 hours.

5 cups diced muskmelon (kharbooja)
2 cups sliced strawberries
5 to 6 tablespoons sugar

For the garnish
sliced strawberries

1. Blend all the ingredients in a liquidiser into a smooth purée.
2. Pour into 2 to 3 large freezer proof containers to form a 25 mm. (1") thick layer. Freeze for 1½ to 2 hours.
3. Serve scoops of the melon and strawberry ice into individual bowls. Serve immediately, garnished with sliced strawberries.

 Both the strawberies and muskmelon should be fresh and ripe. Even one piece of spoilt fruit could spoil this gelato. Adjust the sugar to your preference.

ZUCCOTO

Picture on page 112

This is a special dessert from Florence. The shape of the dessert is said to resemble the dome of Florence's famous church, the Duomo.
Rum soaked sponge cake strips lined a glass bowl, sandwiched with an awfully rich chocolate cream and filled a lemon and fruit flavoured ice-cream. Deep frozen and cut into wedges and served just by itself!
You can use brandy or any liqueur instead of rum if you prefer.
You can prepare the zuccoto a day in advance and keep it frozen until you are ready to serve.
A great way to finish a splendid Italian dinner!

 Preparation time : 15 minutes.   Cooking time : 30 minutes.   Serves 6 to 8.
Setting time : 3 hours.

For the sponge cake
½ can (400 grams for full can) condensed milk
140 grams self-raising flour
1 level teaspoon baking powder
½ teaspoon soda bi-carb
60 ml. melted butter or margarine
1 teaspoon vanilla essence

For the chocolate sauce
¼ cup fresh cream
½ cup chopped dark chocolate

To be mixed into a soaking syrup
3 tablespoons sugar
2 tablespoons rum
3 tablespoons water

To be mixed into a filling
500 ml. vanilla ice-cream
¾ cup walnuts and glace cherries, chopped
2 teaspoons lemon rind, grated

¼ cup toasted almonds, finely chopped

For the chocolate sauce
1. Heat the cream in a pan.
2. Remove from the fire, add the chocolate and mix well to get a smooth sauce.
3. Allow to cool completely.

For the sponge cake
1. Sieve the flour, baking powder and soda bi-carb together.
2. Mix the flour mixture, condensed milk, melted butter, vanilla essence and 75 ml. of water and mix well.
3. Pour the mixture into a greased and dusted 150 mm. (6") diameter tin.
4. Bake in a pre-heated oven at 200°C (400°F) for 10 minutes. Then reduce the temperature to 150°C (300°F) and bake for a further 15 minutes.
5. The cake is ready when it leaves the sides of the tin and is springy to touch when ready, remove from the oven and leave for 1 minute. Invert the tin over a rack and tap sharply to remove.
6. Cool the cake and cut into strips of 25 mm. x 125 mm. (1" x 5").

How to proceed
1. Spread a spoonful of the chocolate sauce on the sponge cake strip. Sandwich with another cake strip. Repeat for the remaining cake strips and chocolate sauce.
2. Line a deep glass bowl with these sponge strips in such a way that is covers the entire bowl leaving a cavity in the centre (as shown in the diagram below).
3. Keep aside 2 to 3 strips to cover the top.
4. Soak the lined sponge with the soaking syrup generously and fill the cavity with the filling mixture.
5. Cover with the remaining sponge slices and soak them with the syrup.
6. Cover with cling film and freeze for 2 to 3 hours.
7. Cut into wedges and serve immediately.

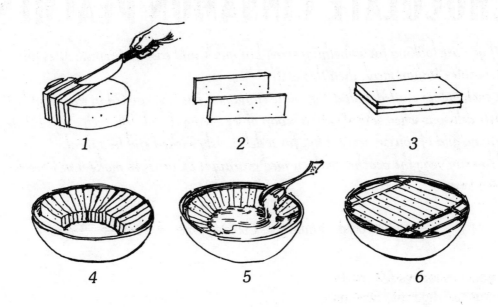

1   2   3

4   5   6

CHOCOLATE CINNAMON PEACHES

If you are looking for something sweet but quick and easy to prepare after an elaborate Italian meal, then this is it!

Peach halves stuffed with a chocolate cinnamon mixture cooked in wine and butter taste delicious when served with a scoop of ice-cream. Cook this recipe just before serving and of course, serve it hot for a deliciously wicked end to a meal.

You can vary the peaches with canned pineapple or pears to make a new recipe each time.

 Preparation time : 5 minutes. Cooking time : 8 minutes.   Serves 4.

8 peaches halves (canned)
4 crushed digestive biscuits
1½ tablespoons grated dark chocolate
2 tablespoons honey
½ teaspoon grated orange rind (optional)
¼ teaspoon cinnamon powder
1 tablespoon cream
¾ cup white wine
1 teaspoon butter
4 scoops vanilla ice-cream to serve

1. Combine the crushed biscuits, chocolate, honey, orange rind, cinnamon powder and cream in a bowl and mix well.
2. Fill the cavities in the peach halves with this mixture, mounding it up slightly.
3. Melt the butter in a large non-stick pan, arrange the stuffed peaches in the pan with the stuffed side facing upwards and pour the white wine over the peaches. Cover with a lid.
4. Cook on a very slow flame for about 7 to 8 minutes and pour the cooking liquid over the peaches at regular intervals while they are cooking.
   Serve hot with vanilla ice-cream.

CASSATA

Italians are credited for creating yet another famous dessert, the Cassata. The name Cassata literally means "little case" due to its brick shape. Cassata is an ice-cream, shaped like a brick, consisting of layers of ice-creams of different flavours on liqueur soaked sponge. This is the Sicilian version of the dessert.
I have chosen ready-made ice-cream to make a quick dessert. You may make the ice-cream yourself at home as shown in the recipe on page 130.
Rum steeped sponge cake, topped with a layer of strawberry ice-cream, flavoured rum soaked sultanas, candied peel, finally topped with coffee cinnamon ice-cream and garnished with grated chocolate. You can prepare the cassata upto 2 to 3 days in advance and keep it frozen.
A great dessert for a great evening!

Preparation time : 15 minutes. No cooking.   Serves 4.
                                Setting time : 7 hours.

For the first layer
½ recipe sponge cake, page 121
1 tablespoon powdered sugar
2 tablespoons rum

For the second layer
250 ml. vanilla ice-cream
4 tablespoons rum
2 tablespoons sultanas
2 teaspoons candied peel, chopped
1 tablespoon roasted almonds, chopped
2 teaspoons strawberry crush

For the third layer
250 ml. coffee ice-cream or vanilla ice-cream mixed
with 1 teaspoon of instant coffee powder, dissolved
in 1 teaspoon warm water
⅛ teaspoon cinnamon powder

For the garnish
grated chocolate

For the first layer
1. Line the sponge cake on the base of a 125 mm. (5") diameter glass bowl or a freezer proof dish.
2. Mix the powdered sugar and rum with 2 tablespoons of water and soak the sponge with this mixture.

For the second layer
1. Soak the sultanas and candied peel in the rum for about 2 to 3 hours.
2. Mix the vanilla ice-cream with the rum soaked sultanas, candied peel, almonds and strawberry crush.
3. Spread this mixture over the first sponge layer.
4. Freeze for about 3 to 4 hours until the ice-cream is firm.

For the third layer
1. Combine the coffee ice-cream with the cinnamon.
2. Spread this coffee ice-cream mixture on top of the second layer (of ice-cream), cover and freeze till it has set for approximately 3 to 4 hours.
3. Cut into pieces and serve chilled, garnished with grated chocolate.

SICILIAN ORANGE ALMOND CAKE

All Sicilians love desserts and cakes. Citrus fruits and almonds are widely grown and of course largely consumed in Sicily, which is an island in the Mediterranean sea.

I actually ate up a large chunk of this cake the first time I made it. So if you are the one who loves hot freshly baked cakes, you will love this delicious tea-time cake flavoured with orange and almonds.

The use of orange squash gives a concentrated orange flavour to the cake.
It is not totally essential but very helpful if you use it.

 Preparation time : 15 minutes. Cooking time : 40 minutes. Serves 4.

1¼ cups plain flour (maida)
½ teaspoon soda bi-carb
1 level teaspoon baking powder
½ cup powdered almonds
1¼ cups powdered sugar
⅓ cup melted butter
⅓ cup fresh curds, beaten
⅓ cup orange juice
2 teaspoons orange squash
1 teaspoon vanilla essence
butter for greasing

For the garnish
½ cup whipped cream
a few orange segments
1 tablespoon toasted almonds

1. Sieve the flour, soda bi-carb and baking powder together.
2. Combine the flour mixture, powdered almonds and sugar in a bowl and mix well.
3. Mix together the butter, curds, orange juice, orange squash and vanilla essence.
4. Add this to the flour mixture and mix well.
5. Pour this batter into a greased 125 mm. (5") diameter cake tin. Bake in a pre-heated oven at 190°C (375°F) for 35 to 40 minutes or until a knife inserted in the cake comes out clean.
6. Allow the cake to cool completely and unmould.
7. Garnish with the whipped cream, orange segments and toasted almonds. Cut into wedges and serve.

CHOCOLATE RICOTTA TORTE

A favourite Italian dessert of a sinfully rich chocolate cake sandwiched with a fruity ricotta filling topped with coffee cream.
"Ricotta" is a fresh and creamy soft Italian cheese similar to cottage cheese but with a sweeter flavour, ideal for savouries and desserts. I have used freshly made cream cheese instead of ricotta for this recipe which gives very good results. You may need to increase the quantity of cream for the filling if the cream cheese seems too dry. If you like, you can even add fresh fruits in the ricotta filling.

 Preparation time : 15 minutes. Cooking time : 25 minutes. Makes 1 torte.

For the chocolate sponge cake
½ can (400 grams for full can) condensed milk
125 grams self-raising flour
1 tablespoon cocoa
1 tablespoon chocolate powder
1 level teaspoon baking powder
½ teaspoon soda bi-carb
60 ml. melted butter or margarine
1 teaspoon vanilla essence

For the ricotta filling
1 recipe cream cheese, page 144
4 to 5 tablespoons powdered sugar
½ teaspoon vanilla essence
2 to 3 tablespoons cream
2 tablespoons chopped candied peel
2 tablespoons glazed cherries, chopped

For the coffee cream topping
1 cup (200 grams) fresh cream
3 tablespoons icing sugar
1 teaspoon instant coffee powder dissolved in 1 teaspoon warm water

Other ingredients
2 to 3 tablespoons brandy to soak the sponge

For the chocolate sponge cake
1. Sieve the flour, cocoa, chocolate powder, baking powder and soda bi-carb together.
2. Mix the condensed milk, flour mixture, 100 ml. of water, the vanilla essence and melted butter thoroughly.
3. Pour the cake mixture into a greased and dusted 150 mm. or 175 mm. (6" or 7") diameter tin.
4. Bake in a pre-heated oven at 200°C (400°F) for 10 minutes. Then reduce the temperature to 180°C (360°F) and bake for a further 15 minutes.
5. The cake is ready when it leaves the sides of the tin and is springy to touch. When ready, take out from the oven and leave for 1 minute. Invert the tin over a rack and tap sharply to remove the cake.
6. Cool the cake.

For the ricotta filling
1. Transfer the cream cheese into a blender with the sugar and blend till is a smooth mixture.
2. Add the vanilla essence, cream, candied peel and glazed cherries and mix well.
3. Refrigerate till required.

For the coffee cream topping
Combine all the ingredients in a clean bowl and whisk till soft peaks form. Keep refrigerated.

How to proceed
1. Slice the cooled chocolate sponge into 2 equal halves horizontally.
2. Place one half on a serving plate and sprinkle with half the brandy.
3. Spread the ricotta filling mixture on top and sandwich it with the other slice of the chocolate sponge.
4. Soak this half of the sponge with the remaining brandy.
5. Cover the cake with the coffee cream topping and refrigerate for at least 2 hours before serving.
6. Cut into wedges.
   Serve chilled.

CARAMELIZED RUM & RAISIN ICE-CREAM

Ice-cream in one of the traditional dishes of Italy. Everyone eats it and there are numerous Gelato stalls selling an astounding variety of ice-cream flavours, usually served in a cone or sometimes scooped into elegant gelato glasses or even sliced. Freeze this ice-cream in a shallow freezerproof container so that the ice-cream sets quickly. I have blended the semi set ice-cream to get a more smooth and creamy ice-cream.

We have to go a very long way to beat Italian ice-creams. They truly are the best in the world.

 Preparation time : 15 minutes. Cooking time : 20 minutes. Serves 4.
Setting time : 6 to 8 hours.

For the ice-cream
½ litre full fat milk
¾ cup (150 grams) sugar
2 tablespoons cornflour
¾ cup (150 grams) cream
1 tablespoon sugar for caramelizing

For the rum-raisin mixture
¼ cup chopped sultanas
¼ cup rum

For the ice-cream
1. Mix together ¼ cup of milk and the cornflour. Keep aside.
2. Add ¾ cup sugar to the remaining milk and bring it to a boil on a medium flame.
3. Add the cornflour mixture and keep aside.
4. Combine 1 tablespoon of sugar with 1 tablespoon of water in a heavy bottomed pan and allow it to melt on a slow flame. Let the mixture turn golden brown in colour.
5. Gradually add the boiled milk to the caramelised sugar and simmer till the mixture coats the back of a spoon.
6. Cool completely, add the cream and mix well.
7. Transfer into a shallow freezerproof dish and freeze for 4 to 6 hours or till it is slushy.

For the rum-raisin mixture
Soak the sultanas in rum for 4 to 6 hours.

How to proceed
1. Remove the semi-set ice-cream from the freezer and transfer it to a blender.
2. Blend till it is smooth and no crystals remain.
3. Transfer into the freezerproof dish, add the rum-raisin mixture and mix well.
4. Freeze again till it sets completely.

$\boxed{\textit{Variation}}$

CHOCOLATE ALMOND ICE-CREAM

Use 2 tablespoons roasted chopped almonds and 4 tablespoons of chopped dark chocolate instead of the rum and raisin for the above recipe.

SICILIAN CREMES

Italians love their desserts and there is always something special for every occasion. The Sicilians are said to have the sweetest tooth of all and many Italian desserts are thought to have originated there.

This recipe is of a favourite Sicilian biscotti or cookies steeped in alcohol and sandwiched with fruits and cream.

These are soft inside and crisp on the outside. They do not keep very well, so sandwich the biscottis with cream and fruits and eat them up quickly!

 Preparation time : 10 minutes. Cooking time : 20 minutes. Makes 12 to 14.

For the biscotti
1 cup plain flour (maida)
½ teaspoon baking powder
1 teaspoon vanilla essence
¼ cup castor sugar or powdered sugar

¼ cup softened butter
1½ tablespoons cold milk

For the filling
½ cup (100 grams) fresh cream
2 tablespoons icing sugar
¼ teaspoon vanilla essence
2 tablespoons brandy (optional)
½ cup sliced oranges
½ cup strawberries, sliced

For the biscotti
1. Sift the flour and baking powder into a bowl. Add the vanilla essence, castor sugar and lemon rind.
2. Rub the butter into the flour mixture till the mixture resembles bread crumbs.
3. Add the cold milk and gently knead it into a dough.
4. Refrigerate for 15 to 20 minutes.
5. Roll into a 12 mm. (½") thick sheet.
6. Cut into circles using a cookie cutter of 37 mm. (1½") diameter. Re-roll the scraps to get more circles.
7. Place them on a baking tray and bake in a pre-heated oven at 160°C (320°F) for 15 to 20 minutes.
8. Remove and cool on a wire rack.
9. Slice into 2 equal halves horizontally while the biscottis are still warm. Cool completely.

For the filling
1. Combine the cream, sugar and vanilla essence and whisk till soft peaks form.
2. Sprinkle a little brandy on each slice of the biscotti, top with a little cream and some fruit on top.
3. Sandwich with the other slice of the biscotti.
   Serve immediately.

BASIC RECIPES

BASIC PIZZA BASE

This is a traditional recipe for a pizza base using a yeast dough.
You can use fresh or dried yeast whichever is available on hand. For dried yeast, use half the quantity of fresh yeast dissolved in warm water before mixing in the flour. While rolling out the dough, the thickness is quite important. If it is rolled out too thin, the pizza will be hard and brittle, but if the dough is too thick, the pizza will be yeasty and indigestible. A thickness between 6 mm. to 10 mm. is desirable. This recipe can be used for pizzas, calzone, focaccias and even for bread rolls.

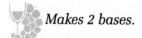 *Makes 2 bases.*

2 cups plain flour (maida)
2 teaspoons (10 grams) fresh yeast, crumbled
1 teaspoon sugar
1 tablespoon olive oil or oil
1 teaspoon salt

1. Combine all the ingredients except the olive oil in a bowl and knead into a soft dough using enough water until it is smooth and elastic (approx. 5 to 7 minutes).
2. Add the olive oil and knead again.
3. Cover the dough with a wet muslin cloth and allow it to prove till it doubles in volume (approx. 15 to 20 minutes).
4. Press the dough lightly to remove the air.
5. Divide the dough into 2 equal parts.
6. Roll each portion into a circle of 250 mm. (10") diameter and 6 mm. (¼") thickness.
   Use as required.

 HANDY TIPS 1. Fresh yeast can be easily purchased from your local bakery in small quantities or you can buy more and store it in the deep freezer.
2. You can also use a ready-made pizza base for any pizza.

NOTE   This pizza base can also be topped with your favourite toppings.

WHOLEMEAL PIZZA BASE

This is a healthier alternative to the basic pizza base as it packs in the goodness of whole wheat flour. Whole wheat flour is used for the dough with either fresh or dried yeast, whichever is more convenient. But when using dried yeast, use ½ the quantity of fresh yeast dissolved in warm water. Be sure to knead the dough very thoroughly until the dough is springy, smooth and elastic.

Pizzas do not necessarily have to be round. Some are large ovals, some are square and others known as pizzettes are baked as smaller individual circles. So you can shape the pizza base the way you like!

 *Makes 2 bases.*

2 cups whole wheat flour (gehun ka atta)
2 teaspoons (10 grams) fresh yeast, crumbled
1 teaspoon sugar
2 tablespoons olive oil or oil
1 teaspoon salt

1. Combine all the ingredients except the olive oil in a bowl and knead into a soft dough using enough water until it is smooth and elastic (approx. 5 to 7 minutes).
2. Add the olive oil and knead again.
3. Cover the dough with a wet muslin cloth and allow it to prove till it doubles in volume (approx. 15 to 20 minutes).
4. Press the dough lightly to remove the air.
5. Divide the dough into 2 equal parts.
6. Roll each portion into a circle of 250 mm. (10") diameter and 6 mm. (¼") thickness.
   Use as required.

POLENTA BASE

An innovative pizza base made using polenta which is a cornmeal porridge that is the traditional dish of Northen Italy. Corn has been a staple in the regions surrounding Venice. Italians have eaten cornmeal polenta for centuries. It is a favourite substitute for bread or pasta. I have used freshly made polenta in a yeast dough to make a delicious pizza base!

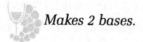 *Makes 2 bases.*

For the polenta
6 tablespoons maize flour (makai ka atta)
½ teaspoon chilli powder
2 teaspoons butter
salt to taste

Other ingredients
1½ cups plain flour (maida)
2 teaspoons (10 grams) fresh yeast, crumbled
1 teaspoon sugar

For the polenta
1. Put ¾ cup of water to boil along with the butter, chilli powder and salt.
2. When the water boils, add the maize flour and mix well with a wooden spoon or whisk.
3. Cook for some time on a low flame, whisking continuously all the time till the mixture thickens.
4. Remove from the fire and cool.

How to proceed
1. Sieve the flour, add the prepared polenta, yeast, sugar and enough water to make a soft dough. Knead till it is smooth and elastic (approx. 5 to 7 minutes).
2. Cover with a wet muslin cloth and allow it to prove till it doubles in volume (approx. 15 to 20 minutes).
3. Press the dough lightly to remove the air.
4. Divide the dough into 2 equal parts.

5. Roll each portion into a circle of 250 mm. (10") diameter and 6 mm. (¼") thickness.
   Use as required.

HANDY TIP Maize flour is made by coarsely milling dried corn. Maize flour or cornmeal is coarse, grainy and pale yellow in texture. In India, we refer to it as makai ka atta.

FRESH PASTA DOUGH

This is a basic recipe to make lasagne and cannelloni sheets, tortellini, ravioli, fettuccine or tagliatelle.

You can make a plain pasta dough or flavour it with herbs or vegetable purée to get a herb pasta or spinach pasta.

The prepared pasta dough must be kneaded very well to make the rolling of pasta simpler. The firmer the dough is, the better the pasta will be.

The pasta dough can be used and cooked as soon as it is made or wrapped in plastic film and refrigerated for upto 2 days.

Preparation time : 10 minutes. Cooking time : 10 minutes. Serves 4.

1 cup plain flour (maida)
4 tablespoons olive oil or oil
¼ teaspoon salt

1. Combine all the ingredients in a bowl and knead into a very firm but smooth dough using very little water.
2. Rest the dough under a wet muslin cloth for 15 minutes and use as required.

Variations

WHOLE WHEAT PASTA DOUGH

Use ½ cup plain flour (maida) and ½ cup whole wheat flour (gehun ka atta) instead of 1 cup plain flour.

VEGETABLE PASTA DOUGH

Add 2 tablespoons of either tomato, carrot, spinach or beetroot purée to the fresh pasta recipe. You may not require water whilst kneading the dough.

FLAVOURED PASTA DOUGH

Flavour fresh pasta dough by adding any of the following ingredients to the above recipe

1 tablespoon mixed herbs (parsley, thyme, oregano, chilli flakes)
1 tablespoon crushed peppercorns
1 tablespoon garlic paste
8 to 10 saffron strands, rubbed in 1 tablespoon of warm milk.

HANDY TIPS 1. For **lasagne**, the pasta should be rolled to suit the size of the
            serving dish.
            2. For **fettuccine**, the pasta sheet should be rolled out thinly
            and cut into 6 mm. (¼") strips.

HOW TO COOK PASTA

The secret of cooking pasta is to use plenty of water. Cooked pasta should be 'al dente' or "firm to the bite". Undercooked pasta is undesirable and has a taste of raw flour, whereas overcooked pasta will be soft and sticky.
Generally speaking, fresh pasta will take about 2 to 5 minutes to cook. Fresh pasta does not increase much in volume whilst cooking as it does not absorb much water.

 Preparation time : Nil. Cooking time : 5 to 10 minutes. Makes 3 cups.

2 cups dried pasta (penne, spaghetti, fusilli, conchiglie, fettuccine, macaroni, dried lasagne sheets)
1 tablespoon oil (for cooking)
1 tablespoon oil (for tossing)
1 teaspoon salt

1. Boil plenty of water in a large pan with 1 teaspoon of salt and 1 tablespoon of oil.
2. Add the pasta to the boiling water by adding a few strands or one sheet of pasta at a time.
3. Cook uncovered, stirring occasionally and gently until the pasta is tender. Cooking times may vary with the size and the thickness of the pasta. Very small pasta (like macaroni, fusilli, conchiglie, penne) may cook in 5 to 7 minutes, while larger shapes (like spaghetti, fettuccine, dried lasagne sheets) may require 10 to 12 minutes.
4. Immediately drain the cooked pasta into a sieve or a colander. Transfer to a bowl of cold water to refresh it. Drain again and keep aside.
5. If the pasta is not to be used immediately, add 1 tablespoon of oil to it and toss it.

P I Z Z A   S A U C E

A classic Italian recipe. This is a blend of harmonious flavours of ripe tomatoes with onion, peppercorns and oregano.

I often make large quantities of this sauce when tomatoes are in season and freeze it in an air-tight container. That way I am always ready to serve pizza in a hurry. You can use this recipe for a pasta sauce. Dilute the sauce using water and add 2 tablespoons of fresh cream to mellow the sauce a little and toss cooked pasta in it. You can add your favourite herbs too, like a few leaves of basil.

 Preparation time : 10 minutes. Cooking time : 25 to 30 minutes. Makes approx. 1 cup.

4 large tomatoes
2 bay leaves
4 to 6 peppercorns
1 small onion, chopped
1 teaspoon garlic, chopped
½ capsicum, deseeded
2 tablespoons tomato purée (optional)
¼ cup tomato ketchup
1 teaspoon sugar
½ teaspoon dried oregano

2 tablespoons olive oil or oil
salt to taste

1. Blanch the tomatoes in boiling water.
2. Peel, cut into quarters and deseed the tomatoes.
3. Chop finely and keep the tomato pulp aside.
4. Heat the olive oil, add the bay leaves and peppercorns and sauté for a few seconds.
5. Add the onion, garlic and capsicum and sauté for a few minutes.
6. Add the tomato pulp and allow it to simmer for 10 to 15 minutes until the sauce reduces a little.
7. Add the tomato purée, ketchup, sugar and salt and simmer for some more time.
8. Finally, add the oregano and mix well. Remove the capsicum, bay leaves and peppercorns and discard.
   Use as required.

P E S T O

A traditional recipe with the distinct flavours of fresh basil, pine nuts, garlic and olive oil. Pesto appears in many form throughout Italy as a sauce for pasta, a salad dressing, a pizza sauce or to aromatise a hot bowl of soup. Pine nuts (chilgoza) are another ingredient that is used in pesto to give it a nutty flavour. In its absence, you can substitute it with walnuts. The ingredients are pounded together to make a thick paste, using a pestle, hence the name "Pesto".
For a pasta sauce, you need to dilute the pesto using milk and cream as shown in the recipe on page 92.
Pesto is best when it is freshly made. But if you wish to refrigerate it, top with a thin layer of olive oil and it can then be refrigerated in an air-tight container for upto 2 weeks.

 Preparation time : 5 minutes. Cooking time : 5 minutes. Makes ½ cup.

¼ cup pine nuts (chilgoza) or walnuts, chopped
2 cups fresh basil leaves, loosely packed

2 tablespoons olive oil
1 teaspoon chopped garlic
salt to taste

1. Lightly roast the pine nuts. Cool completely.
2. Combine all the ingredients in a blender and blend into a smooth paste.
3. Use as required.

Variation

CLASSIC ITALIAN PESTO

Add ¼ cup of parmesan cheese at step 2 and follow the same method.

HANDY TIP Ready to use pesto is also available in bottles at gourmet stores.

SUN-DRIED TOMATO PESTO

Pesto appears in many dishes throughout Italy, although the Basil Pesto is more popular all over. The sun-dried tomato pesto is popularly used all along the Mediterranean regions.

Sun drenched tomatoes, walnuts, olive oil and garlic is the combination for this pesto. The ingredients are ground together to make a thick paste either using a mortar and pestle or in a blender. The Italians serve this pesto topped on breads or with their pasta and for piquant salad dressings.

The pesto needs to be thinned down with milk and cream if it used as a pasta sauce. You can make larger quantities of this recipe and refrigerate it.

Preparation time : 5 minutes. Cooking time : 5 minutes. Makes ½ cup.

¼ cup pine nuts (chilgoza) or walnuts
¼ cup sun-dried tomatoes, page 142, soaked
2 tablespoons olive oil
1 teaspoon chopped garlic

1 teaspoon chilli powder
salt to taste

1. Lightly roast the pine nuts. Cool completely.
2. Combine all the ingredients in a blender and grind to a smooth paste.
3. Use as required.

 If you use sun-dried tomatoes which are preserved in oil, you need not add the olive oil as mentioned in the recipe.

SUN-DRIED TOMATOES

A great way to preserve tomatoes. Sun-dried tomatoes are salty, chewy and tangy in taste. They impart a sharp concentrated tomato flavour to pizza and pasta recipes. Ready-made sun-dried tomatoes are also available both dry and also preserved in olive oil. If you are using sun-dried tomatoes soaked in olive oil, you do not need to soak them in water.

 Makes ¾ cup (100 grams).

2 kg. firm red tomatoes
4 tablespoons sea salt (khada namak)

1. Wash and wipe the tomatoes.
2. Cut the tomatoes into quarters.
3. Toss the tomatoes with the salt, place on a sieve in a single layer and leave to dry under the sun.
4. When the sun sets, cover the sieve with a muslin cloth and bring it indoors.
5. Repeat for 6 to 7 days till the tomatoes dry out completely.
6. Store the sun-dried tomatoes in an air-tight container.
7. Soak in a little warm water for about 5 minutes and use as required.

EGGLESS MAYONNAISE

This is a modified version of the classic mayonnaise sauce, substituting eggs with condensed milk.

It tastes great when combined with pesto as a salad dressing as used in the Pesto Pizza Sandwich, recipe on page 53.

You can make larger quantities of this sauce and refrigerate it.

It stays well for upto a week when refrigerated.

 Preparation time : a few minutes. No cooking.   Makes 1 cup.

½ can (400 grams for full can) condensed milk
4 tablespoons salad oil
4 tablespoons white vinegar or lemon juice
½ teaspoon salt
1 teaspoon mustard powder
½ teaspoon pepper powder

1. Gradually, mix all the ingredients together using a whisk. Store in a refrigerator.
2. Use as required.

 HANDY TIP   You can also buy ready-made eggless mayonnaise which has a longer shelf life.

CREAM CHEESE

 Preparation time : a few minutes. Cooking time : 10 minutes. Makes 1½ cups (approx.)

1 litre full fat milk
1 teaspoon citric acid crystals
½ cup warm water

1. Put the milk to boil in a thick bottomed pan.
2. When it comes to a boil, remove from the flame and keep aside for a few minutes.
3. In another bowl, mix the citric acid crystals with the warm water.
4. Pour this mixture into the hot milk and allow it to stand for about 5 minutes till the milk curdles on its own. Stir gently if required.
5. Strain this mixture using a muslin cloth.
6. Blend the drained milk solids in a food processor till thick and creamy. Use as required.

 If the drained whey is milky, boil it once more and strain the separated milk solids.